Cambridge Certificate in Advanced English 4

WITH ANSWERS

Examination papers from the University of Cambridge Local Examinations Syndicate

CAMBRIDGE
UNIVERSITY PRESS

PUBLISHED BY THE PRESS SYNDICATE OF THE UNIVERSITY OF CAMBRIDGE
The Pitt Building, Trumpington Street, Cambridge, United Kingdom

CAMBRIDGE UNIVERSITY PRESS
The Edinburgh Building, Cambridge CB2 2RU, UK
40 West 20th Street, New York, NY 10011–4211, USA
477 Williamstown Road, Port Melbourne, VIC 3207, Australia
Ruiz de Alarcón 13, 28014 Madrid, Spain
Dock House, The Waterfront, Cape Town 8001, South Africa

http://www.cambridge.org

First published 1999
Fourth printing 2004

Printed in the United Kingdom at the University Press, Cambridge

ISBN 0 521 65651 6 Student's Book
ISBN 0 521 79765 9 Student's Book with answers
ISBN 0 521 65652 4 Teacher's Book
ISBN 0 521 65653 2 Set of 2 Cassettes

Contents

Thanks and acknowledgements

The publishers are grateful to the following for permission to reproduce copyright material. It has not always been possible to identify the sources of all the material used and in such cases the publishers would welcome information from the copyright owners.

Elle for the texts 'Mauritius' and 'France' by Susan Ward-Davies and A. P. Watt Ltd for the text 'New Zealand' by Jan Morris on p. 5; *The Independent* for the article by Robert Richardson on p. 8; *Marie Claire* for the texts on pp. 11–12, © Marie Claire/IPC Magazines Ltd; *BBC Wildlife Magazine* for the article by Dr Jared Diamond on pp. 32–3; *The Economist* for the article on pp. 34–5, © The Economist, London (3/10/92); Cambridge City Council Leisure Services for the texts on pp. 37–8; *Cosmopolitan* for the article on p. 57, Cosmopolitan September 1991, © National Magazine Company; *The Independent on Sunday* for the article by Esther Oxford on pp. 58–9 and for the article by Colin Tudge on pp. 60–1; *Which?* for the article on pp. 63–4. *Health Which?* is published by the Consumers' Association, 2 Marylebone Rd, London NW1 4DF (for further information telephone 0800 252100); Macmillan for the text on p. 86 from *Extraordinary People* by Derek Wilson.

Text permissions by Sophie Dukan.

Photographs (black and white): Pictor International for p. 34.

Colour section: (t) = top, (b) = bottom, (l) = left, (r) = right, (m) middle (all pages viewed in portrait format)
Photographs: Pictor International Ltd for pp. C1 (t), C2 (bl) and (ml), C7 (b); Mary Evans Picture Library for p. C1 (b); Gettyone Stone for pp. C2 (tr), C12 (t); Telegraph Colour Library for pp. C2 (tl) and (br), C4 (b), C7 (t), C9, C12 (m) and (b), C13, C16; Rebecca Watson for p. C2 (mr); Famous/Peter Aitchison for p. C4 (t); The Image Bank for p. C5; Rex Features Ltd for pp. C11, C14.
Artwork: UCLES/Gecko Ltd for pp. C3, C5, C6, C15.

Picture research by Diane Jones and Rebecca Watson

Design concept by Peter Ducker [M S T D]

Cover design by Dunne & Scully

The cassettes which accompany this book were recorded at Studio AVP, London.

To *the student*

This book is for candidates preparing for the University of Cambridge Local Examinations Syndicate (UCLES) Certificate in Advanced English (CAE) examination. It contains four complete tests based on past papers which have been adapted to reflect the most recent CAE specifications (introduced in December 1999).

The CAE examination is part of a group of examinations developed by UCLES called the Cambridge Main Suite. The Main Suite consists of five examinations which have similar characteristics but which are designed for different levels of English language ability. Within the five levels, CAE is at Cambridge Level 4.

Cambridge Level 5 Certificate of Proficiency in English (CPE)
Cambridge Level 4 Certificate in Advanced English (CAE)
Cambridge Level 3 First Certificate in English (FCE)
Cambridge Level 2 Preliminary English Test (PET)
Cambridge Level 1 Key English Test (KET)

The CAE examination consists of five papers:

Paper 1	**Reading**	1 hour 15 minutes
Paper 2	**Writing**	2 hours
Paper 3	**English in Use**	1 hour 30 minutes
Paper 4	**Listening**	45 minutes (approximately)
Paper 5	**Speaking**	15 minutes

Paper 1   Reading

This paper consists of four parts, each containing one text or several shorter pieces. The texts are taken from newspapers, magazines, non-literary books, leaflets, brochures, etc., and are selected to test a wide range of reading skills and strategies. There are between 40 and 50 multiple matching, multiple-choice and gapped test questions in total.

Paper 2   Writing

This paper consists of two writing tasks (e.g. letter, report, review, instructions, announcement, etc.) of approximately 250 words each. **Part 1** consists of one compulsory task based on a substantial reading input. **Part 2** consists of one task selected from a choice of four. Question 5 is always business related. Assessment is based on content, organisation and cohesion, accuracy and range of language, register and effect on target reader.

Paper 3   English in Use

This paper consists of six tasks designed to test the ability to apply knowledge of the language system, including vocabulary, grammar, spelling and punctuation, word-building, register and cohesion. It contains 80 items in total.

Paper 4   Listening

This paper consists of four texts of varying length and nature which test a wide range of listening skills. There are between 30 and 40 matching, completion and multiple-choice questions in total.

Paper 5   Speaking

Candidates are examined in pairs by two examiners, one taking the part of the Interlocutor and the other of the Assessor. The four parts of the test, which are based on visual stimuli and verbal prompts, are designed to elicit a wide range of speaking skills and strategies from both candidates.

Candidates are assessed individually. The Assessor focuses on grammar and vocabulary, discourse management, pronunciation, and interactive communication. The Interlocutor provides a global mark for the whole test.

Marks and results

The five CAE papers total 200 marks, after weighting. Each paper is weighted to 40 marks.

Your overall CAE grade is based on the total score gained in all five papers. It is not necessary to achieve a satisfactory level in all five papers in order to pass the examination. Certificates are given to candidates who pass the examination with Grade A, B or C. A is the highest. The minimum successful performance in order to achieve Grade C corresponds to about 60% of the total marks. You will be informed if you do particularly well in any individual paper. D and E are failing grades. If you fail, you will be informed about the papers in which your performance was particularly weak.

The CAE examination is recognised by the majority of British universities for English language entrance requirements.

Further information

For more information about CAE or any other UCLES examination write to:

EFL Division
UCLES
1 Hills Road
Cambridge
CB1 2EU
England

Telephone: +44 1223 553311
Fax: +44 1223 460278
e-mail: efl@ucles.org.uk
http://www.cambridge-efl.org.uk

Test 1

Paper 1 Reading (1 hour 15 minutes)

Part 1

Answer questions **1–15** by referring to the magazine article on page **5**.

Indicate your answers **on the separate answer sheet**.

For questions **1–15** answer by choosing from paragraphs **A–H** on page **5**. You may choose any of the paragraphs more than once.

Note: When more than one answer is required, these may be given **in any order**.

Which hotel(s)

is the owners' home?	1	
are not luxurious?	2	3 ....
offer mountain views?	4	5 ....
includes participation in leisure activities in its price?	6	
is so pleasant that guests may stay longer than planned?	7	
is said to be attractive on account of its simplicity?	8	
are in buildings which originally had a different function?	9	10 ....
looks like hotels found in another country?	11	
is described as being in a most unusual location?	12	
has not been well maintained?	13	
currently attracts a new type of guest?	14	
is said to be untypical of hotels in that part of the world?	15	

REMOTE HOTELS

A INDIA
GHANERAO HOTEL, RAJASTHAN

Ghanerao Hotel sits at the edge of the Aravalli Hills in a small rural village dominated by craftsmen. It mixes English country-house tranquillity with Indian symbolism. The Ghanerao family have lived there for 400 years and today, Sajjan Singh and his wife have opened their home to paying guests. The facilities are basic, with hot water arriving by bucket, but the spartan aspects of life at Ghanerao just add to its appeal.

B NEW ZEALAND
HERMITAGE HOTEL, MOUNT COOK

One of my favourite hotels is the Hermitage Hotel on New Zealand's South Island which I came across by chance when I was climbing. We had been flown up to near the top of a glacier and had climbed to the peak and then had to walk all the way down. When we finally reached the bottom, to my astonishment, there was this hotel. It was on its own in the most stupendously beautiful countryside, very wild and very high up. To come down the mountain battered and exhausted and find yourself in extreme luxury, with a man playing Cole Porter on the piano, was extraordinary.

C MAURITIUS
BEACHCOMBER PARADIS HOTEL

On the south-west of Mauritius, the Paradis Hotel is isolated on its own peninsula in one of the quietest corners of the island. If you drive from here, the road winds along the coast past beaches with no-one on them but fishermen. The hotel isn't small and there are plenty of takers for the free watersports, but you can easily escape from all the other people along nine kilometres of private beach; you have only to swim a few yards out into the Indian Ocean and you can barely see the hotel for palm trees. Sit on the beach in the evening when everyone has gone and as the light drains from the sky you'll feel far away from everything.

D ST LUCIA
LADERA HOTEL, ST LUCIA

The Ladera Hotel in St Lucia has one of the Caribbean's most dramatic settings. Quiet and far off the beaten track, it stands at an altitude of 1,000 feet, its open rooms looking out between the twin peaks of the Pitons to the Caribbean Sea - some view first thing in the morning! The style is colonial, with furniture in mahogany and greenheart wood, and four-poster beds screened with muslin netting.

E TURKEY
THE SPLENDID HOTEL, INSTANBUL

This hotel, on Büyükada in the Princes Islands is the perfect place to escape the noise of Istanbul. The islands are only an hour by boat, and are simply idyllic. There are no cars, only horse-drawn carriages and fabulous twenties wooden architecture. The islands are a cross between Key West and the Old South, and the landmark building is the Splendid. All in wood, painted white with red domes, it's a copy of a turn-of-the-century hotel on the French Riviera. Today it's a little run down, but has lost none of its charm.

F FRANCE
CHATEAU D'ETOGES, EPERNAY

In the tiny village of Etoges, in the heart of Champagne, is a beautiful seventeenth century château. Surrounded by a moat with two swans, the château, until recently a family home, has 20 rooms which are all different, some with four-poster beds - one even has a large billiard table. There are special weekend rates for two nights with breakfast and dinner plus complimentary champagne (their own brand - if you want to take some home).

G KENYA
THE FAIRVIEW HOTEL, NAIROBI

The Fairview is that rare bird in Africa - a comfortable hotel that hasn't decked itself out in feathers of upmarket gloss and tasteless luxury. It's an indispensable staging post, always full of travellers recuperating from one safari and planning the next. Overnight guests have been known to arrive, take one look at the gardens, the bedrooms and the dining-hall menu, and decide on the spot to stay for a week. There are even apartments set aside specially for those who make up their minds to settle in for a few months. The hotel's leafy acres and scattered buildings are laid out on Nairobi Hill, a world away from the overhead bustle of the city centre. I don't know of any better place to sit and watch the sudden African sunset, sipping draught beer and looking forward to a hearty dinner - braised zebra and two veg, following by jelly trifle.

H ITALY
HOTEL SPLENDIDO PORTOFINO

The Duke of Windsor was the first to sign the visitor's book at the Hotel Splendido. Ever since, a galaxy of the fabulous has drifted in and out of the hotel's portals to play, stay and be seen: Lauren Bacall and Humphrey Bogart, Liz Taylor and Richard Burton. Nowadays, you are more likely to find yourself in the company of a soft drinks billionaire or a rubber-tyre heiress. But this old Monastery-turned-villa-turned-hotel is still, as its name suggests, quite splendid and there is enough reflected glamour to perk up any weekend break. Deliciously simple food in the restaurant and the finest Persian rugs and homemade pasta.

Part 2

For questions **16–22**, you must choose which of the paragraphs **A–H** on page **7** fit into the numbered gaps in the following newspaper article. There is one extra paragraph which does not fit in any of the gaps.

Indicate your answers **on the separate answer sheet**.

Life was getting out of hand

__Susan Harr__ unplugs her gadgets and rediscovers the joys of manual labour

Everyone is in love with technology. It gives us all those marvellous gadgets that make life easier and leave us so much more time to do other things. A gradual, though not particularly subtle, form of brainwashing has persuaded us that technology rules, and that it is OK.

| 16 |

However, a recent unhappy experience with my malfunctioning word processor – a £48 call-out fee, a labour charge of £15 per quarter of an hour, plus parts and replacements costs – has confirmed a suspicion that gadgets are often not worth the expense or the trouble. Are we as dependent on technology as we imagine? Bit by bit, I have been letting the household technology fall by the wayside as its natural and often short life expires.

| 17 |

So when the thing started making curious noises, which continued even when it was disconnected by a puzzled service agent, I abandoned it to the backyard, where it whispers damply to itself like some robot ghost.

| 18 |

Of course, there are some gadgets I would not like to be without. A year living without a washing machine convinced me of the value of the electric washtub. But there are others whose loss has brought unexpected delight. Feeling that we were becoming too apt to collapse in front of the television, or slot in a video, I sent back the rented colour equipment and we returned to the small black-and-white portable.

| 19 |

One of these, in my own case, is sewing; and here is another gadget that went by the board. My old *Singer* sewing machine is now an ornamental plant table, and as I cannot afford to replace it, I have taken to sewing by hand.

| 20 |

In fact, the time I now spend placidly stitching is anything but tedious, and the advantages are numerous. For a start, I can sew and listen to the radio – another rediscovered pleasure – or I can talk with family and friends. If it

is a simple task, I can watch the programmes I do want to see on television, and alleviate my puritanical guilt at sitting in front of the box by doing something useful at the same time. And what a lovely, cosy feeling it is to sit by the fire and sew with a pot of tea for company.

| 21 |

There is a wonderfully soothing quality about executing a craft by hand, a great satisfaction in watching one's work become neater, more assured. I find things get done surprisingly quickly, and the pace of life suddenly slows down to the rhythm of my own hands. I am also freed from one of the most detestable aspects of late 20th century life – the need to rush to finish an activity so that I can rush to the next.

| 22 |

The result of all this brooding is that I now prowl the house with a speculative eye. Do we *really* need the freezer, the microwave oven, that powered lawn-mower? Come to think of it, we could save an awful lot of money by doing without electric lights!

A It is a real strain on the eyes and concentrates the mind on what is really worth watching. We now spend a lot more time walking the dog (who never liked television anyway), reading, talking or pursuing other hobbies.

B First to go was the dishwasher. I had always felt that by the time we had collected enough dishes for a worthwhile load, put in the soap and the rinse aid, emptied the filter of the disgusting gunge it collected and filled it with special salt, I could have done the lot by hand.

C This makes me wonder just what 'time' technology gives us. The time to take up more activities for which we must buy more gadgets? If so, hats off to the marketing experts: but I think they are conning us.

D Quite wrongly, I had tended to think with horror of the women who sewed elaborate garments, robes, linen and household items by hand. I thought of those long hours, the strain on the eyes and so on.

E These implications are obvious. The movement of my fingers uses nothing from the previous power supply being eaten up by our greedy race. A craft executed by hand does not pollute the environment.

F I am not tied to a noisy, whirring machine, with my head bent and my back turned on the world, and I can take my time over the garment. In any case, I was always slightly alarmed by those electric machines that dash across the fabric towards your fingers. Best of all, I can pop the whole lot into a carrier bag and take it with me wherever I go.

G Meanwhile I have regained control of my sink, where I plunge my hands into the suds and daydream while doing the washing up – an agreeable, if temporarily forgotten, activity.

H We have come to believe that we could not do without it, and if we do resist the notion that our lives would be unmanageable without the appliances of science, we certainly do not want to relinquish them. Pity the generations whose lives were blighted by tedious and blister-inducing toil. Even our brains are relieved of exertion by computers that not only perform miraculous calculations with amazing speed, but now provide entertainment.

Part 3

Read the following article from a magazine and then answer questions **23–27** on page **9**. On your answer sheet, indicate the letter **A, B, C** or **D** against the number of each question **23–27**. Give only one answer to each question.

Indicate your answers **on the separate answer sheet**.

Ordinary people, ordinary lives

Most of us have photographs of our grandparents, but how many of us know what their lives were like, the sort of people they were in their youth? The glimpses rare diaries give us are frustratingly incomplete, family anecdotes only half remembered. And what will our grandchildren know about us? We often intend to write things down, but never get round to it. We may leave videos rather than photographs, but the images will remain two-dimensional.

Hannah Renier has come up with an answer: she writes other people's autobiographies, producing a hardback book of at least 20,000 words – with illustrations if required – a chronicle not of the famous, but of the ordinary.

The idea came to her when she talked to members of her family and realised how much of the past that was part of her own life was disappearing.

"When I started I didn't take it nearly so seriously as I do now, having met people who genuinely will talk and have led interesting lives," she says. "They would say they are doing it for their children or for posterity, but they are getting quite a lot out of it themselves. They enjoy doing it."

The assurance of confidentiality encourages her subjects to overcome any instinct of self-censorship.

"I had the confidence to be honest," says a 62-year-old man who made and lost one fortune before making another. "I was surprised at what came out. There were things that hurt, like my divorce, and the pain was still there."

"I did it for my family, so that perhaps they could learn something, but I have

not yet let my children – who are in their thirties – read it. They were hurt by things in my life and there are a lot of details which I don't feel I want them to know at the moment. If they insist, I'll let them. But I think I'd rather they read it after I was dead."

He also recognised patterns laid down in childhood, which showed themselves in repeatedly making the same mistakes. It is something Ms Renier has detected in other people. "It's amazing how many people really have been conditioned by their parents," she says. "The injunctions and encouragements that were laid down in childhood have effects for the rest of their lives. They become caught in repeating patterns of behaviour. They marry the sort of people of whom their parents approved – or go in the opposite direction as a sort of rebellion."

"A lot of disappointments come out. Sixty years later they still are regretting or resenting things that were never resolved with their parents. There is no age of reason. If people had hang-ups in their youth, they still have them in middle age. They live their lives in an attempt to impress a parent who wasn't impressed and if that fails some of them seem to be seeking permission to say 'I can't stand my mother'."

Recorder rather than inquisitor, Ms Renier keeps her distance. "It's not for public consumption and I'm not there as a very nosy person. People have got carried away and told me something, then said, 'I'm not sure if that ought to go in'. I put it in anyway – they can remove things when they see the draft. But generally people want to be honest, warts and all."

"It's not vanity publishing, it's not people saying 'Gosh, I've had such an interesting life the world's got to know about it.' Things are moving much faster than at any time in history and we are losing sight of what happened in the past. It's a way of giving roots. We need some sort of link to our ancestors because people don't sit around in an extended family any more. People want a little immortality."

Each book involves up to 30 hours of taped interviews which Ms Renier uses as the basis to write the life story, rearranging the chronology and interpreting. Modern technology allows her to produce everything except the binding with its gold lettering: choose your own colour of library buckram, pick your own title.

Fascinating to the private audience at which each book is aimed, the results are obviously not of the dirt-at-any-cost school of life story. Ms Renier organises her material logically and writes well; the final content is as good as its subject. The book that emerges does not look like a cheap product – and carries a price tag of nearly £3,000, with extra copies at £25 each. She receives about 10 inquiries a week, but the cost – inevitable with the time involved – clearly deters many people.

"I thought it would be a more downmarket product than it is," she says. "But the people I've done have all been county types, readers of Harpers & Queen, which is one of the magazines where I advertise. They're the sort of people who at one time would have had their portraits painted to leave to their descendants."

23 According to the writer, most people
  A have no interest in leaving records for their grandchildren.
  B are unable to find out much about their grandparents.
  C find stories about their grandparents' families boring.
  D want their grandchildren to know only good things about them.

24 Hannah Renier decided to write other people's autobiographies because
  A she had already done so for relatives.
  B she had met so many interesting people.
  C she wanted to preserve the past.
  D she had often been asked to do so.

25 The 62-year-old man asked her to write his autobiography
  A so that he could reveal his true feelings.
  B because his family wanted to read it.
  C so that his children would understand him.
  D because he thought he was close to death.

26 Hannah is surprised that many of her subjects
  A regret the marriages they made.
  B remain influenced by their parents.
  C refuse to discuss their childhoods.
  D want to be like their parents.

27 The autobiographies that Hannah produces
  A follow exactly what she was told by her subjects.
  B are intended to be interesting to anyone.
  C look less expensive than they really are.
  D present the facts in a way that is easy to follow.

Part 4

Answer questions **28–45** by referring to the magazine article on pages **11–12**, in which various women are interviewed about their jobs.

Indicate your answers **on the separate answer sheet.**

For questions **28–45**, match the statements on the left below with the list of women **A–E**. You may choose any of the women more than once.
Note: When more than one answer is required, these may be put **in any order**.

She accepts failure as an inevitable part of her job.	**28**	
She has to make sure that regulations are being obeyed.	**29**	
It is very important that she gives people the right instructions.	**30**	
She dislikes some of the people she deals with.	**31**	**A** THE BRAIN SURGEON
She has to be available for contact outside working hours.	**32** **33**	**B** THE SENIOR DESIGNER
She sometimes eats and works at the same time.	**34** **35**	**C** THE CHAUFFEUR
She finds that every day is differently organised.	**36**	**D** THE LANDSCAPE GARDENER
She sometimes refuses to answer questions.	**37**	
She feels she needs more time for a particular aspect of her work.	**38**	**E** THE CIVIL ENGINEER
She sometimes makes decisions independently.	**39**	
She finds it difficult to stop thinking about her job.	**40** .... **41** **42**	
She values the approval of her customer.	**43**	
Her comments on other people's work may be resented.	**44**	
She obtains most of her work by following up earlier jobs.	**45**	

Take Five Careers

Rebecca Cripps meets five women who discuss their different professions: the highlights, the drawbacks and their typical working day

A THE BRAIN SURGEON
Name: Anne
Age: 34
ANNE'S DAY

"I get up at 6.30am, go the gym at 7am, get to work by 8am and start operating at 8.30am. I operate all Monday and Wednesday, as well as some Friday afternoons. Most standard head operations take three hours, but some operations take all day. I've worked ten hours straight through on occasion without eating or going to the loo.

Deciding when to operate, and what to do, can be stressful. I don't feel particularly stressed when operating, but sometimes I worry about what I'm going to do the next day. Brain surgery tends to be a last resort for a patient, but when it works it's tremendous, and more than makes up for the unsuccessful times. From 10am to 1pm I hold an out-patients' clinic, when I explain the operations. I enjoy this and find it quite easy to talk to the patients. If they get upset, I comfort them, but time pressure can make this difficult.

I leave work between 6pm and 8pm. Some nights and weekends I'm on call, and I always carry my bleeper. On holidays, I worry for the first three days about the people I've left behind, and at night I dream I'm operating. I'm hopeless at switching off."

B THE SENIOR DESIGNER
Name: Marita
Age: 31
MARITA'S DAY

"I get up at 7.45am, leave the house by 8.20am, take the train to work and arrive at 9.15am. At 10.30am on Monday we meet to discuss what we're doing, any problems or whether anyone needs help. We work in teams – in my team there are three senior designers, a company partner who oversees everything, and a junior designer. The work usually involves ten to fifteen per cent design: the rest is production. I'll be given a brief by the client – with luck the company will have clear ideas about what they want to say, their target market and the form of the project. I then spend three or four weeks designing, researching and developing the project.

After this I present my ideas to the client and once they've agreed to them, we work out estimates and budgets, and I start commissioning photographers and illustrators. I liaise with the printers and make sure the needs of the job are being met, and on time. I spend a lot of time managing people. I have to be able to communicate with a broad range of people, and briefing them correctly is essential. When their work comes in, I assemble everything and send it to the printers. Keeping several jobs going at once can send stress levels sky-high. Deadlines are always looming, and no day has a set structure. Lunch is at 1pm for an hour, when we try to get out to the pub. Otherwise I have sandwiches and work through. It's a great feeling if the client gives a good response to the designs you've done and you know the project has worked; it's a great disappointment when you've worked really hard and the job gets rejected. I get home at 7.30pm at the earliest; often it's 8.30pm and sometimes much later. I find it hard to unwind when I get back, especially if I'm very busy."

C THE CHAUFFEUR
Name: Linda
Age: 42
LINDA'S DAY

"I get up at about 7am most days, but two or three mornings a week I meet a long-haul flight from Heathrow or Gatwick and get up between 4.30am and 5am. At 10.30 or 11am I might go for a bike ride, or swim. Because chauffeuring is a sedentary job, I have to watch my diet and exercise quite carefully. I usually have a big breakfast, though, and just have snacks during the day. People often ask me to recommend restaurants, nightclubs or shops, so I have to know my way around. Luckily, a lot of the jobs are pre-booked, so I get a chance to look routes up beforehand. Not everyone is polite. Some passengers are anti-social, some arrogant, some downright rude. But most of the time people are very well behaved and I've built up a good rapport with my regular clients.

There are times when I hear a conversation in the car and have to make sure my eyes are firmly on the road and my ears shut. Sometimes the press have tried to make me talk about clients I've carried, but I won't. I work a seven-day week, up to fifteen hours a day. I have to be careful not to get too tired. I try to get to bed by 11pm."

D THE LANDSCAPE GARDENER
Name: Tracy
Age: 27
TRACY'S DAY
"I get up at about 7am, leave the house at 7.30am and get to my first job. My assistant and I spend most of our time maintaining gardens we originally designed and landscaped. We do a few commercial jobs but most of our work is in private gardens. We spend about an hour and a half at each house. At about 11am we get hungry and go to a local cafe for a big breakfast. I often look at my watch and wish it was earlier and that time didn't pass so quickly. In summer I may work until 10pm; in winter until 4.30pm.

The business office is at home, so when I get back I listen to any messages and respond to any calls. If someone wants their garden landscaped, I'll usually arrange a consultation with them in the evening – at about 7pm or 8pm. We specialise in using old materials, such as old bricks and unusual plants, to make gardens look as if they were built a long time ago. But sometimes people have a set idea of what they want, and it can be pretty horrible. Still, it's very satisfying when we do a complete landscape from start to finish and then see all the blooms come out.

It's hard to relax in the evenings because I can always hear the business line when it rings. I never have any trouble sleeping because the work I do is so physical that I'm always exhausted at the end of the day. I wouldn't say I'm very strong, but I'm fit. Physically, it's a very tough job, but it does let your imagination run wild."

E THE CIVIL ENGINEER
Name: Zena
Age: 27
ZENA'S DAY
"I arrive at the site by 8.30am. I'm assistant resident engineer at the site, so I'm looking after the building of a couple of bridges and a retaining wall – which prevents people driving off the road into a quarry. I check that the contractors are working to the schedule and specifications, with correct safety systems and minimum environmental impact. I help to co-ordinate the site professionals and find solutions to any problems.

The contractors start work at 6am, so my first task is to find out from the clerk of works what's been going on since I left the night before. The rest of the day is a reaction to whatever he tells me. Usually there's some paperwork from the contractors to look at, or there might be design queries to answer. Lunch is usually for half an hour between 2pm and 2.30pm, but I tend to grab things to eat as I go along. The contractors have set mealtimes and when they're off eating it's easier to check things on site. Because we're checking their work it can cause conflict, so our relationship has to be as open as possible. I see the duty resident engineer once a day. However, if something really important comes up I don't wait to tell them before I act. I usually leave the site at about 6pm and I'm on call all the time."

PAPER 2   WRITING (2 hours)

Part 1

You **must** answer this question.

1   While on holiday in New Zealand, you were very upset when you lost your backpack. You reported this to the police. Now, some time later, you are back home and, to your amazement, you receive through the post your backpack with all its contents **except your passport**, together with an unsigned note.

Read the Missing Articles statement below and the note on page **14**. Then, using the information provided, write the **two letters** listed on page **14**.

NEW ZEALAND POLICE

MISSING ARTICLES – Statement

Description of article(s):
1 large, green backpack with badges from Japan, Bali and Australia.

Contents:
1 35 mm camera in black case and 3 rolls of used film
1 passport – No. O-H-65839
1 red leather address book
Various items of clothing
1 1999 diary
Various toiletries.

Where last seen:	Auckland bus station
Date reported:	14.04.99
Reference:	MG/JEB/148

> 2 May 1999
>
> *Found this backpack hidden under a bush near the beach in Auckland. I hope nothing is missing!*
>
> *Your name and address were at the front of the address book.*
>
> *All the best!*

Now write:

(a) a **letter** to the Editor of the *Auckland News*, describing what happened, and conveying your thanks to the person who found your backpack; you would also like to repay the cost of sending the backpack to you (about 200 words)

(b) a **brief letter** to the New Zealand police containing relevant information about the returned backpack (about 50 words).

You do not need to include addresses. You should use your own words as far as possible.

Part 2

Choose **one** of the following writing tasks. Your answer should follow exactly the instructions given. Write approximately 250 words.

2   The magazine published by your English club has been encouraging readers to exchange information about books they have enjoyed reading in English. The books can be of any type (not only literature). Write a short **review** including a brief summary of a book which you have enjoyed reading, saying why you think others might enjoy it and what they might learn from it.

3   You have been invited to write an article for PROJECT 2000, an international magazine which covers interesting and important developments throughout the world. The article must draw readers' attention to and raise interest in the main challenge faced by young people in your country at the start of the twenty-first century.

Write the **article**.

4   A British film company would like to make a 30-minute video for tourists about your town. You have been invited to submit proposals stating:

- what places the video should show and why
- who it would be interesting to have interviewed on the video and why
- what is special about the character of your town that the video should try to convey.

Write your **proposal**.

5   Your company or organisation is considering the possibility of setting up a branch or office in another country but has not yet decided where the best place to establish itself would be. You have been asked to write a report recommending a location which you feel would be suitable.

Write the **report**, naming the location you have chosen and explaining why you feel it would be suitable. Refer to relevant factors such as geographical position, potential for recruiting staff, communications and any other important features.

PAPER 3   ENGLISH IN USE (1 hour 30 minutes)

Part 1

For questions **1–15**, read the article below and then decide which word on page **17** best fits each space. Put the letter you choose for each question in the correct box on your answer sheet. The exercise begins with an example (**0**).

Example:

0	B		0

FRIDAY THE THIRTEENTH

Police are hunting for a hit-and-run driver who knocked a teenage cyclist off her bike in East Street. Sarah Tucker, 17, had a lucky **(0)** ..... on Friday, 13th May, when she was sent reeling by a black Volvo on her way home from work.

She bruised her thigh and shoulder and her bicycle was **(1)** ..... . The driver stopped for a moment but then drove off without **(2)** ..... a name or address and before Sarah could get his number. "I tried to **(3)** ..... out of his way, but I couldn't," she said. "Everyone at work kept **(4)** ..... on about it being Friday 13th. I'm not a bit **(5)** ..... and wouldn't change any of my plans just because Friday 13th is supposed to be unlucky, I don't usually take any **(6)** ..... of that sort of thing but I will now. I think I'll stay in bed."

The accident **(7)** ..... at the **(8)** ..... with Westwood Road at about 6.30pm as Sarah was making her **(9)** ..... home to the Harley Estate.

The Volvo **(10)** ..... out of Westwood Road onto Henley Road in front of the teenager's bicycle. "He could at **(11)** ..... have helped her up. I don't see why he should get away with it," said her father, Derek. "Sarah was lucky. I don't know why the driver didn't see her. He can't have been **(12)** ..... attention. It is **(13)** ..... that nobody took down the number." Though still too **(14)** ..... to ride a bike, Sarah was able to go back to **(15)** ..... in Marlow on Monday.

0	**A**	break	**Ⓑ**	escape	**C**	escapade	**D**	incident
1	**A**	crashed	**B**	harmed	**C**	devastated	**D**	damaged
2	**A**	leaving	**B**	presenting	**C**	noting	**D**	suggesting
3	**A**	go	**B**	get	**C**	be	**D**	stay
4	**A**	chatting	**B**	running	**C**	going	**D**	rambling
5	**A**	irrational	**B**	prejudiced	**C**	unreasonable	**D**	superstitious
6	**A**	notice	**B**	consideration	**C**	note	**D**	care
7	**A**	took place	**B**	came about	**C**	finished up	**D**	turned up
8	**A**	junction	**B**	joining	**C**	roundabout	**D**	crossing
9	**A**	route	**B**	course	**C**	way	**D**	path
10	**A**	pulled	**B**	thrust	**C**	ran	**D**	crashed
11	**A**	once	**B**	least	**C**	most	**D**	best
12	**A**	paying	**B**	giving	**C**	attracting	**D**	providing
13	**A**	unfavourable	**B**	inopportune	**C**	undesirable	**D**	unfortunate
14	**A**	discouraged	**B**	shaken	**C**	overcome	**D**	confused
15	**A**	work	**B**	post	**C**	job	**D**	employment

Part 2

For questions **16–30**, complete the following article by writing the missing words in the correct box on the answer sheet. **Use only one word for each space**. The exercise begins with an example **(0)**.

Example:

0	*any*	0

ALLERGIES

Put simply, an allergy is a disorder in which the body over-reacts to harmless substances which in normal circumstances should not produce any reaction at all. An allergy can occur in almost **(0)** ..... part of your body, and can **(16)** ..... caused by just about anything. Mainly **(17)** ..... , allergies become evident on parts of the body directly exposed **(18)** ..... the outside world. Certain allergies occur only at certain times of the year, while **(19)** ..... are there all the time. Those **(20)** ..... occur all the year round are probably caused by something you come into contact **(21)** ..... every day of your life, some seemingly harmless object **(22)** ..... as your deodorant **(23)** ..... the pillow you lie on each night. Allergies can occur at any time during your life, **(24)** ..... usually do so before your fortieth birthday. Sometimes the symptoms are **(25)** ..... slight you do not even know you have an allergy, and it may take years **(26)** ..... an allergy to become noticeable. It all depends **(27)** ..... the amount of the substance to **(28)** ..... you are exposed and for how **(29)** .... Sometimes an allergy can disappear as **(30)** ..... as it arrived, without any treatment. Sometimes it comes and goes for no apparent reason, and with no regularity.

Part 3

In **most** lines of the following text, there is **one** unnecessary word. It is either grammatically incorrect or does not fit in with the sense of the text. For each numbered line **31–46**, find this word and then write it in the box on your answer sheet. **Some lines are correct.** Indicate these with a tick (✓) in the box. The exercise begins with two examples **(0)** and **(00)**.

Examples:

0	✓		0
00	the		0

BOB TISDALL

0   In the early part of the 20th century, Bob Tisdall became famous by

00   the winning four events in just two hours in a university athletics

31   competition. He won the 400 metres, the 100 metres hurdles, the

32   long jump, and putting the shot. Because of at that time university

33   athletics made it the front page of national newspapers, and as

34   Tisdall was extremely handsome, he became very well-known.

35   He was offered to parts in films and attractive jobs in business

36   but he was more interested in seeing round the world and he

37   took up a position in India. He forgot about sport for a while but

38   then someone reminded him about that the Olympics were taking

39   place soon in four months' time. He decided to have a go and went

40   to Los Angeles, where he represented for Ireland in the 400 metres

41   hurdles. Although it was not only the third time he had competed

42   in this event, he won it with a record-breaking time of 51.7 seconds.

43   This is remarkable if we could compare Tisdall's training with

44   the intense training that modern athletes undergo to prepare them

45   for the Olympics. Tisdall's 'training' consisted of staying in bed for

46   a week, going straight out from his bed to the track – and winning!

Part 4

For questions **47–61**, read the two texts on pages **20–21**. Use the words in the boxes to the right of the text, listed **47–61**, to form a word that fits in the same numbered space in the text. Write the new word in the correct box on your answer sheet. The exercise begins with an example **(0)**.

Example:

0	immediately	0

EXTRACT FROM A MAGAZINE

FIVE WAYS TO IMPROVE YOUR MEMORY

- Pay better attention at the time. Rehearse the information **(0)** ..... afterwards, allowing **(47)** ..... longer gaps between each **(48)** ..... . Thus, when you hear a name, say it to yourself, then say it again a minute later, and so on.

- Tax your brain in a **(49)** ..... of ways. One researcher found that rats given interesting things to do had better memories than 'bored' rats.

- Attach meaning to memory – the more **(50)** ..... an event is, the better it will be remembered.

- Attach what you want to remember to something already familiar to you. Let's say you need to remember ten words: start by **(51)** ..... things that are well known to you **(52)** ..... , such as objects in your house, then associate one of the words with each.

- Have confidence in your ability to remember things. Don't **(53)** ..... your brain.

(0)	**IMMEDIATE**
(47)	INCREASE
(48)	REPEAT
(49)	VARY
(50)	SIGNIFY
(51)	MEMORY
(52)	PERSON
(53)	ESTIMATE

MUSEUM LEAFLET

SUPPORTING THE MUSEUM'S WORK	
Behind the scenes at the museum, over three hundred **(54)** ..... are engaged in vital research into areas of **(55)** ..... significance, addressing issues such as water pollution, tropical disease, and the management of **(56)** ..... systems. Research at the museum is partly funded by your **(57)** ..... fee, but if you would like to make an **(58)** ..... donation, please do so. You can also support our work with a Museum Credit Card. Please complete an application form at the Information Desk. A further way to support our work is to become a member of the Museum by paying a small annual **(59)** ..... fee. The advantages of **(60)** ..... include free entry, a free magazine, considerable **(61)** ..... on prices in the Museum Shop and an exclusive programme of special events.	**(54)** SCIENCE **(55)** GLOBE **(56)** ECOLOGY **(57)** ADMIT **(58)** ADD **(59)** SUBSCRIBE **(60)** MEMBER **(61)** REDUCE

Part 5

For questions **62–74**, read the following job advertisement and use the information in this text to complete the numbered gaps in the informal letter. Then write the new words in the correct spaces on your answer sheet. **Use no more than two words for each gap**. The words you need **do not** occur in the advertisement. The exercise begins with an example **(0)**.

Example:

0	looking for	0
		— —

JOB ADVERTISEMENT

MARKETING DIRECTOR

An exceptional individual is sought to succeed the present director, Ms Jane Fairbrother, who will be vacating the post in the new year to take up a new appointment in Edinburgh.

The successful applicant will ideally be a university graduate in Business Administration and have the ability to take charge of the department in a period of rapid change. Experience in a company that manufactures similar products would be a distinct advantage. Applicants must demonstrate a proven record of success. The Marketing Director is responsible for a department of over 30 staff and the position entails a considerable amount of overseas travel.

Benefits include generous leave (42 days p.a.), a subsidised canteen, and a range of sporting and social facilities. Salary is negotiable according to experience.

Please e-mail your application with full career details to:
Phillipa.Robertson@intelect.com.uk
The closing date is 30 November.

INFORMAL LETTER

You know I promised to tell you if I heard of any interesting jobs going? Well, our company is **(0)** ..... a new Marketing Director – the ad goes in next week.

The new director will be **(62)** ..... from Jane Fairbrother, who's leaving because she's been **(63)** ..... a new job in Scotland. Since you have **(64)** ..... in Business Administration you'll stand a good chance. I can just see you as the **(65)** ..... of the department. You are working in the same **(66)** ..... (which is what they want) and you have done **(67)** ..... in your present job that they are bound to be impressed. If you get the job, you'll have more than 30 people **(68)** ..... and you would have to make a number of **(69)** ..... . The holidays you get are **(70)** ..... , and the canteen food is edible and doesn't **(71)** ..... . As for the money they will pay, you will have to **(72)** ..... with them – it **(73)** ..... your experience. Your application must **(74)** ..... by 30 November, so get your skates on!

Love

Margaret

Part 6

For questions **75–80**, read the following text and then choose from the list **A–J** the best phrase given below to fill each of the spaces. Write one letter **(A–J)** in the correct box on your answer sheet. Each correct phrase may only be used once. **Some of the suggested answers do not fit at all.** The exercise begins with an example **(0)**.

Example:

0	J		0

ENGLISH SPELLING

English was first written down in the 6th century. At that time, writers had to use the twenty-three letters of the Latin alphabet **(0)** ..... . Because English has sounds that do not exist in Latin, they added letters **(75)** ..... . This resulted in some irregular spelling. After the Norman invasion of England in 1066, French became the language spoken by the king and other people in positions of power and influence. Many French words were introduced and the spelling of many English words changed **(76)** ..... . The result was a rich and irregular mix of spellings.

The printing press was invented in the 15th century. Many early printers of English texts spoke other first languages, especially Dutch. They often paid little attention **(77)** ..... . Sometimes technical decisions were made **(78)** ..... . To do this, letters were taken off the ends of words and sometimes added to words. With time, people became used **(79)** ..... . Fixed spellings were therefore created by the printers' decisions. Spoken English, however, was not fixed. It continued **(80)** ..... . It is no wonder that English spelling seems irregular. Words such as although, through and cough, for example, all have the same spelling at the end, but are pronounced differently. Words such as feet, meat and seize, on the other hand, are spelled differently but have the same sound in the middle.

A to have a great influence
B to seeing words spelled in the same way
C to follow French patterns
D to change, as it still does
E to show the spellings
F to influence the French
G to how English words were spelled
H to represent the forty-four sounds of English
I to give columns of print straight edges

J to write down what they heard

PAPER 4   LISTENING (45 minutes approximately)

Part 1

You will hear a talk about a product called Akwaaba sauce. For questions **1–10**, complete the notes.

You will hear the recording **twice**.

Akwaaba sauce

The recipe was originally from	India
Mr Ford and Mr Stott worked at	**1**
They went into business in	**2**
It is now the only sauce of its kind that can be described as	**3**
The High Lama was given some sauce because he was	**4**
The ingredients come from	**5**

the Mediterranean and India.

The recipe for the sauce is known by	**6**
Each vat in the factory contains	**7** of the sauce.
Each of the ingredients is kept separately for	**8**
It is made in a bottle with a	**9**
The bottle is made of	**10**

Part 2

You will hear an announcement about a change in transport arrangements. For questions **11–18**, complete the notes the speaker is using.

Listen very carefully as you will hear the recording ONCE only.

DESTINATION: Portsmouth

DEPART: [_____ 11]

JOURNEY TIME: [_____ 12]

OTHER INFORMATION: Reassure passengers that the relief ferries are

[_____ 13]

COMPENSATION:

(i)   Free   [_____ plus ____ 14]

(ii)   SEEWAYS pay   [£   per   15]

(NB cabin surcharge will be   [_____ 16])

(iii)   MEDWAY INSURANCE will pay £10 for   [_____ 17]
waited.

(iv)   Passengers will need to show   [_____ 18]   in order
to collect compensation.

Part 3

You will hear a woman on a radio programme interviewing a driving instructor about his job. For questions **19–26**, choose the correct answer **A, B, C** or **D**.

You will hear the recording **twice**.

19 People want to pass the driving test quickly because
    A they are impatient.
    B they are nervous about it.
    C they don't want to spend too much.
    D they find lessons time-consuming.

20 Fred's driving school gets customers because
    A it has a nationwide reputation.
    B people trust Fred to get them through the test.
    C people tell their friends about it.
    D he has a friendly personality.

21 Fred prepares learners for their lesson by
    A telling them not to be nervous.
    B encouraging them to relax.
    C talking about their last lesson.
    D talking calmly to them.

22 Fred suggests new drivers are nervous because
    A they don't get enough practice.
    B they are worried about road conditions.
    C they forget where the controls are.
    D their reactions are slower.

23 Fred allows his pupils to drive unaided when
    A they are in complete control.
    B they can handle the car quite well.
    C they understand how the gears work.
    D they are sufficiently relaxed.

24 According to Fred, good drivers tend to be
    A decisive people.
    B overconfident.
    C those who enjoy driving.
    D patient.

25 Fred says that for a driver, intellectual ability is
    A becoming increasingly important.
    B likely to reinforce self-confidence.
    C less important than being practical.
    D more important than a good memory.

26 According to Fred, driving is becoming more
    A difficult.
    B sophisticated.
    C expensive.
    D efficient.

Part 4

You will hear various people talking about the experience of winning something.

You will hear the recording **twice**. While you listen you must complete **both tasks**.

TASK ONE
For questions **27–31**, match the extracts as you hear them with the people listed **A–H**.

A	unemployed person	
B	cook	**27**
C	artist	**28**
D	author	**29**
E	parent	
F	horse trainer	**30**
G	gardener	**31**
H	retired person	

TASK TWO
For questions **32–36**, match the extracts as you hear them with the topics listed **A–H**.

A	cookery competition	**32**
B	an award-winning design	**33**
C	playing golf	
D	chess championship	**34**
E	prize-winning short story	
F	general knowledge quiz	**35**
G	prize-winning vegetables	**36**
H	photographic competition	

PAPER 5   SPEAKING (15 minutes)

There are two examiners. One (the Interlocutor) conducts the test, providing you with the necessary materials and explaining what you have to do. The other examiner (the Assessor) will be introduced to you, but then takes no further part in the interaction.

Part 1 (3 minutes)

The Interlocutor will first ask you and your partner a few questions. You will then be asked to find out some information about each other, on topics such as hobbies, interests, career plans, etc.

Part 2 (4 minutes)

You will each be given the opportunity to talk for about a minute, and to comment briefly after your partner has spoken.

   The Interlocutor gives you a set of photographs and asks you to talk about them for about one minute. Each set of photographs has a different focus, so it is important to listen carefully to the Interlocutor's instructions. The Interlocutor then asks your partner a question about your photographs and your partner responds briefly.

   You will then be given another set of photographs to look at. Your partner talks about these photographs for about one minute. This time the Interlocutor asks you a question about your partner's photographs and you respond briefly.

Part 3 (4 minutes)

In this part of the test you and your partner will be asked to talk together. The Interlocutor will place a new set of pictures on the table between you. This stimulus provides the basis for a discussion. The Interlocutor will explain what you have to do.

Part 4 (4 minutes)

The Interlocutor will ask some further questions, which will lead to a more general discussion of what you have talked about in Part 3 and in which you will be encouraged to comment on what your partner says.

Test 2

Paper 1   Reading (1 hour 15 minutes)

Part 1

Answer questions **1–14** by referring to the book reviews on page **31**.

Indicate your answers **on the separate answer sheet.**

For questions **1–14** answer by choosing from the reviews of books for teenagers **A–G** on page **31**.

Note: When more than one answer is required, these may be given **in any order.**
    Some choices may be required more than once.

According to the reviews, which book or books

features a character who cannot be trusted?	**1**	
feature a major change in lifestyle?	**2**	**3** ....
highlights a potentially violent situation?	**4**	
have characters searching for evidence?	**5**	**6** ....
shows the pleasure people derive from animals?	**7**	
exploit a variety of sources to tell the story?	**8**	**9** ....
contain elements that should make people smile?	**10**	**11** ....
features a child who has a difficult relationship with a parent?	**12**	
is described as equally suited to both sexes?	**13**	
is about a girl who takes up an unusual hobby?	**14**	

Hide and Seek
Yvonne Coppard

Emma and her friends are pursuing a holiday game – surveillance of a suspicious bookshop – when she realises that one of its rare customers is her Uncle Jim.

He callously draws her into a web of deceit and crime, manipulating her affection for him and attempting to alienate her from her friends, whose characters are persuasively drawn by Coppard.

When Emma finds her life in danger, things take a dark and compelling turn – her confinement in the cellar of a derelict house is stunningly handled.

This book reveals the minutiae of family life, the bonds of childhood friendship and warns that adults aren't always the protectors they ought to be. A vital and convincing read.

Backtrack
Peter Hunt

Two teenagers, 'peasant' Jack and Rill, a boarder at a posh girls' school, join forces on realising that relatives of both were involved in an apparently inexplicable 1915 train accident, in which eight people died. Varied viewpoints and documents – maps, first-hand accounts, court records, railway histories – throw an ever-changing light on the incident, so that the reader works as hard as the two protagonists to understand what happened and why. A clever, complex novel which rewards close attention.

Pigeon Summer
Ann Turnbull

Mary Dyer doesn't really fit into her family or male-dominated culture; for one thing, she, a girl, loves her father's racing pigeons and when he must go away to find work, Mary knows enough to carry on managing the loft and winning prizes, despite increasing conflict with her harassed mother. Set believably in 1930, this readable tale has a sound basic message that 'There are different kinds of cleverness', which can't be bad. Thoughtful readers should find satisfaction here.

Yaxley's Cat
Robert Westall

Unusually, Robert Westall uses the viewpoint of a mature woman for this chilling story of rural prejudice and persecution. Rose, to escape from her materialistic life and her smug husband, rents Sepp Yaxley's cottage with her two children. A ferocious cat, and bizarre items found in cupboards, reveal the answer to why Yaxley disappeared; but the newcomers' presence arouses local hostility to the point where their own lives are at risk. By the end, the threatening violence is controlled, but Rose feels just as dismayed by the methodical ruthlessness of her teenage son. Utterly gripping.

Someone's Mother is Missing
Harry Mazer

At the poor, shambling, noisy end of the family there's Sam – fat, overtalkative and awed by his supercool and sophisticated cousin, Lisa, from the apparently rich end of the clan. When Lisa's privileged world crumbles, it's Sam who helps her to find some balance, out of which both gain a better sense of reality and the value of family.

The pace is slightly slow in parts but there's a gentle humour and the developing closeness of the two teenagers is convincingly handled. It could be interesting to both boys and girls, which is a bit of a rarity.

Stanley's Aquarium
Barry Faville

Barry Faville writes with assurance and humour, vividly evoking his New Zealand setting and creating an intelligent and likeable first-person narrator. Robbie takes a job gardening for elderly Stanley, finding him at first fascinating and later repellent; when she finds out what he keeps in his aquarium and what he plans to do with them, the book takes a 'thrillerish' twist without losing its sharp insight into character and relationships. Unusual and compelling.

Dodger
Libby Gleeson

A painful, sad story where the troubled personal relationships plus the stormy school life of Mick are told through a skilful blend of flashback, a teacher's letters to a friend, the boy's own notes and sympathetic narrative. Coming to terms with the negative expectations of others and his own poor sense of self-worth is achieved through a role in a school play and by an impressively sensitive first-year teacher.

Highly recommended, even though it's truly an agonising read, especially at the end.

Part 2

For questions **15–20**, you must choose which of the paragraphs **A–G** on page **33** fit into the numbered gaps in the following magazine article. There is one extra paragraph which does not fit in any of the gaps.

Indicate your answers **on the separate answer sheet**.

NATURAL TALENTS

In the mere seven million years since we humans separated from chimpanzees, we haven't had time to develop any differences: genetically we're still more than 98 per cent identical to chimps.

15

That's a large burden to place on a relative handful of genes. It should come as no surprise, then, that modern studies of animal behaviour have been shrinking the list of attributes once considered uniquely human, so that most differences between us and animals now appear to be only matters of degree.

16

The earliest art forms may well have been wood carvings or body painting. But if they were, we wouldn't know it, because those materials don't get preserved. Not until the Cro-Magnons, beginning around 35,000 years ago, do we have unequivocal evidence for a distinctly human art, in the form of the famous cave paintings, statues, necklaces and musical instruments.

17

First, as Oscar Wilde said, "All art is quite useless". The implicit meaning a biologist sees behind this quip is that human art doesn't help us survive or pass on our genes – the evident functions of most animal behaviours. Of course, much human art is utilitarian in the sense that the artist communicates something to fellow humans, but transmitting one's thoughts or feelings isn't the same as passing on one's genes. In contrast, birdsong serves the obvious functions of defending a territory or wooing a mate, and thereby transmitting genes. By this criterion human art does seem different.

18

As for human art's third distinction – that it's a learned rather than an instinctive activity – each human group

does have distinctive art styles that surely are learned. For example, it's easy to distinguish typical songs being sung today in Tokyo and in Paris. But those stylistic differences aren't wired into the singer's genes. The French and Japanese often visit each other's cities and can learn each other's songs. In contrast, some species of birds inherit the ability to produce the particular song of their species. Each of those birds would sing the right song even if it had never heard the tune. It's as if a French baby adopted by Japanese parents, flown in infancy to Tokyo and educated there, began to sing the French national anthem spontaneously.

19

Yet even connoisseurs would mistake the identity of two mid-twentieth century artists named Congo and Betsy. If judged only by their works, they would probably be identified as lesser-known abstract expressionists. In fact the painters were chimpanzees. Congo did up to 33 paintings and drawings in one day, apparently for his own satisfaction, and threw a tantrum when his pencil was taken away.

20

These paintings by our closest relatives, then, do start to blur some distinctions between human art and animal activities. Like human paintings, the ape paintings served no narrow utilitarian functions; they were produced not for material regard but only for the painter's satisfaction. You might object that human art is still different because most human artists intend their art as a means of communication. The apes, on the other hand, were so indifferent to communicating with other apes that they just discarded their paintings. But that objection doesn't strike me as fatal, since even some human art that later became famous was created by artists for their private satisfaction.

A   Perhaps we can now explain why art as we usually define it – the dazzling explosion of human art since Cro-Magnon times – burst out spontaneously among only one species, even though other species may be capable of producing it. Since chimps do, in fact, paint in captivity, why don't they do so in the wild? I suggest that wild chimps still have their days filled with problems of finding food, surviving, and fending off rivals. If the ancestors of wild chimps had more leisure time, chimps today would be painting. Indeed, some slightly modified chimps – we humans – are.

B   The role of learning in human art is also clear in how quickly our art styles change. Roman authors described geese honking 2,000 years ago, as geese still do today. But humans innovate so rapidly that even a casual museum-goer would recognise almost any twentieth century painting as having been made later than, say, the Mona Lisa. Connoisseurs can do better, of course. When shown a work with which they are not familiar, they can often identify not only when it was painted but who painted it.

C   Congo and Betsy were honoured by a two-chimp show of their paintings in 1957 at London's Institute of Contemporary Art. What's more, most of the paintings available at that show sold; plenty of human artists can't make that boast.

D   On this grand evolutionary scale, whatever it is that separates humans from animals is a very recent development. Our biological history implies that our physical capacity for making art (whatever changes were needed in the human physique, brain, and sense organs) and anything else we consider uniquely human must be due to just a tiny fraction of our genes.

E   If we're going to insist that our recent creative burst finally does set us apart, then in what ways do we claim that our art differs from the superficially similar works of animals? Three supposed distinctions are often put forward: human art is non-utilitarian, it's made for aesthetic pleasure and it's transmitted by learning rather than by genes. Let's scrutinise these claims.

F   For example, tools are used not only by humans but also by wild chimpanzees (which use sticks as eating utensils and weapons), and sea otters (which crack open clams with rocks). As for language, monkeys have a simple one, with separate warning sounds for 'leopard', 'eagle' and 'snake'. These discoveries leave us with few absolute differences, other than art, between ourselves and animals. But if human art sprang from a unique genetic endowment, isn't it strange that our ancestors dispensed with it for at least the first 6.9 million of the 7 million years since they diverged from chimps?

G   The second claim – that only human art is motivated by aesthetic pleasure – also seems plausible. While we can't ask robins whether they enjoy the form or beauty of their songs, it's suspicious that they sing mainly during the breeding season. Hence they're probably not singing just for aesthetic pleasure. Again, by this criterion human art seems unique.

Part 3

Read the following newspaper article and then answer questions **21–25** on page **35**. On your answer sheet, indicate the letter **A, B, C** or **D** against the number of each question **21–25**. Give only one answer to each question.

Indicate your answers **on the separate answer sheet**.

Young Masters

Age is against Bobby Fischer as he seeks again to re-establish himself. Chess is more than ever a young man's game.

After 20 years of self-imposed exile, Mr Bobby Fischer has returned to chess and is playing his old adversary Boris Spassky. Mr Fischer's victory in the first game was a masterpiece, simple but profound. But, as subsequent games have shown, this balding, bearded chess player is not the man of 1972. He is 49 years old, out of practice and out of shape. Mr Spassky is even older.

Chess has also changed a lot over the past two decades. A new era of professionalism was born out of Mr Fischer's own popularisation of the game. The rise of the professional chess circuit has seen the competitive aspect of the game overtake the scientific and artistic. The sole aim of the modern master is to win.

In international chess, a player's nerves and stamina are as crucial as his intellect and wisdom. The pressure of the game has always been intense: a chess clock is used to ensure that each player completes the stipulated number of moves in the allotted time – failure to do so results in immediate loss of the game. But now the playing sessions themselves are becoming longer, and many games are played without a break. The increased pressure has swung the pendulum in youth's favour. Over the past 30 years, each new world champion has been younger than his predecessor. It is significant that, of the world's

ten highest-ranked players, eight are under 30.

Nor is it only the way the game is played that has changed. Much of modern chess is played off the board – and not just the battle for psychological advantage that Mr Fischer wages so well. Every professional must now take seriously his pre-match preparation, not least because the age of computer databases has had a profound impact on chess. A small portable computer can hold one million chess games, and give instant access to hundreds of games of a prospective opponent.

In one recent contest, each of the protagonists employed large teams of assistants to work round the clock searching for flaws in the other's repertoire. The opening stages of a chess game are now analysed to near exhaustion. Simply being better prepared in a chess opening can be the deciding factor in the game.

The chess world today boasts more first-rate players than at any stage in its history. Hundreds of grandmasters chase modest prize money the world over. Success demands physical as well as mental exertion. A single game may last up to eight hours. For the chess master this period represents a ceaseless struggle. A lapse in concentration can mean disaster. So the adversaries are always in a state of nervous tension.

The presence of the chess clock adds to the tension. The climax of the game is often a furious 'time scramble'. When this occurs, each player has only seconds to make several moves or face instant forfeiture. With minds racing and hands twitching, the masters blitz out their moves and press their clocks with a co-ordination that any athlete would admire. Such moments are not for reflective intellectuals. The game descends into a primeval struggle in which nerves, tenacity and an overwhelming will to win separate victor from vanquished.

At the top level of chess, the pain of losing is unbearable. Winning brings immense satisfaction and a chance to recover from the nerves and exhaustion. But one victory is not enough to win a tournament. The chess master must be ready for the struggle the next day. Most chess competitions last for 9–11 days, with play on every day, and there is an all-year-round tournament circuit. World championship matches are even more exacting. The 1984 encounter between Anatoli Karpov and Gary Kasparov in Moscow had to be aborted after several months on the grounds of mutual exhaustion. Mr Karpov had shed around two stone (10kg) in weight.

Can Mr Fischer defy these odds? He once declared "All I want to do, ever, is play chess." This sentiment made his exodus from the chess world after 1972 seem even more inexplicable. But in some respects it was a fitting end to his story. It immortalised Bobby Fischer.

If he has come back for the money, he is onto a good thing. Whatever happens in his match with Mr Spassky, each will end up several million dollars richer. But if Mr Fischer has returned in the sincere belief that he can show he is still the best player in the world, the final result could be heartbreaking.

21 According to the writer, modern chess players are more
    A intelligent.
    B creative.
    C determined.
    D impressive.

22 Why is there more pressure in international chess nowadays?
    A The games are played to a strict time limit.
    B The players are expected to keep going for longer.
    C The games contain more moves than previously.
    D The players do not have breaks in games any more.

23 The modern chess professional must research
    A commercial opportunities.
    B his opponent's strategies.
    C psychological tactics.
    D physical training techniques.

24 The final moves of a loser's game are characterised by
    A rapid responses.
    B angry exchanges.
    C nervous errors.
    D thoughtful play.

25 The difficulties of older players can be attributed to their opponents'
    A physical superiority.
    B greater skill.
    C mental attitude.
    D commercial motivation.

Part 4

Answer questions **26–42** by referring to the information from a brochure on pages **37–38**.

Indicate your answers **on the separate answer sheet.**

For questions **26–42**, match the statements on the left below with the list of places **(A–E)** on the right below. You may choose any of the places more than once.

Note: When more than one answer is required, these may be given **in any order**.

The means of displaying the exhibits has not changed. **26** ....

If you spend some time here, you might produce something of decorative value. **27** .... **28** ....

You can enjoy special privileges by joining this institution. **29** ....

Arrangements can be made to buy copies of the exhibits. **30** ....

The exhibits are arranged chronologically. **31** .... **32** ....

The arrangement of the exhibits saves the visitor time. **33** ....

Experts are employed to provide information and support. **34** .... **35** ....

Visitors have access to reproductions rather than originals. **36** .... **37** ....

The present collection has evolved from a much earlier one. **38** ....

Here you will find the best selection of exhibits of this type in Europe. **39** ....

There is a second exhibition space that contains exhibits with aesthetic appeal. **40** ....

This organisation provides a wide range of learning opportunities. **41** ....

Exhibitions of this type are now rare. **42** ....

A The University Museum of Classical Archaeology

B Cambridge Darkroom

C Sedgwick Museum of Geology

D The Cambridge University Collection of Air Photographs

E Cambridge Medieval Brass Rubbing Centre

A The University Museum of Classical Archaeology

The Museum of Classical Archaeology is one of the few surviving collections of casts of Greek and Roman sculpture in the world, comprising over six hundred works. The first thing to remember about the collection is that nothing here is genuine. All the sculptures are accurate replicas cast from the originals, mostly in the late 19th and early 20th centuries. The Museum is housed in a purpose-built gallery with excellent natural light. The advantages of plaster casts are many: groups of sculptures originally set up together but now split between various museums all over Europe can be viewed together as originally intended. Nearly all the most celebrated works of Greek and Roman sculpture can be viewed in one afternoon.

B Cambridge Darkroom

Cambridge Darkroom is a centre for photography with community darkrooms and a gallery showing a varied exhibition of photography and related media. We regularly run courses and workshops for people of all ages and abilities, including our popular Beginner's Course, a shorter Induction Course and Master Classes with invited photographers. We have a membership scheme whereby all our members can use our darkrooms. We also encourage young photographers (aged 12 to 16) to develop their skills with our Young Members scheme, led by our resident photographer. We stock photographic books and art magazines and carry a full range of photographic materials.

C Sedgwick Museum of Geology

The Sedgwick Museum houses a magnificent collection of fossil animals and plants, rocks and minerals of all geological ages, and from all parts of the world. It also houses Britain's oldest intact geological collection, that of Dr John Woodward (1665–1728). It includes nearly 10,000 rare and interesting specimens stored in their original early 18th century cabinets. Adam Sedgwick was Professor of Geology and keeper of the Woodwardian collection. Throughout his long life, he added enormously to the collections, laying the foundations of a truly outstanding museum. The collection is arranged by geological age so that the major changes in life on Earth can be traced through time.

The new Whewell Gallery houses the beautiful minerals and gems of the collection. The displays are accompanied by full explanatory labels to explain both their nature and modern use.

D The Cambridge University Collection of Air Photographs

There are over 400,000 oblique and vertical air photographs in the collection, taken by members of the university's staff over the past 45 years. The University has its own aircraft based at Cambridge Airport and undertakes photographic work throughout Great Britain. The photographs are of considerable general interest as a detailed, year-by-year record of the landscape, showing both the natural environment and the effects of human activity from prehistoric times to the present day. There is a small display in the entrance hall and the knowledgeable library staff will be happy to deal with particular enquiries. The photographs cannot be borrowed but copies can normally be purchased. These are made to order and ordinarily take about a month.

E | **Cambridge Medieval Brass Rubbing Centre**

Cambridge Brass Rubbing Centre, the second oldest and longest surviving centre in the world, is one of the region's most unusual tourist attractions. Hours of enjoyment are to be had creating wall hangings by rubbing one of over a hundred different brass plates off tombs of medieval knights and ladies. By formulating resin copies, known as facsimiles, the centre has made it possible to preserve the originals and still make brass rubbing an accessible pastime to all. The brass plates, as an alternative means of memorial to the tomb statue, spread from Germany across medieval Europe and Scandinavia. Through various revolutions most of the beautiful brasses were destroyed. The vast majority of remaining brasses are to be found in Britain and the widest range of examples can be seen at the Cambridge Centre.

PAPER 2   WRITING (2 hours)

Part 1

You **must** answer this question.

1   You recently saw an advertisement about work placements abroad. You wrote to your friend Sheila, who lives in Zimbabwe, about the advertisement and she has replied to you.

Read the advertisement below with your queries added to it, and the extract from Sheila's letter on page **40**. Then, using the information provided, write the **two letters** listed on page **40**.

Work Placements Abroad Ltd.

* Want to spend a month working in an English-speaking country?
* Interested in gaining new skills?
* Keen to improve your English?

If so, then apply to us.

We at WPA have a worldwide reputation for arranging short-term work placements in international organisations. We will pay you an allowance which will cover your (living and accommodation expenses,) but you will need to arrange somewhere to stay.

What's reasonable? – ask Sheila

Ask Sheila for advice!

Write and tell us:

* what type of work placement you are looking for;
* when you would be available;
* what academic and/or work experience you have;
* what you think you would gain from this placement.

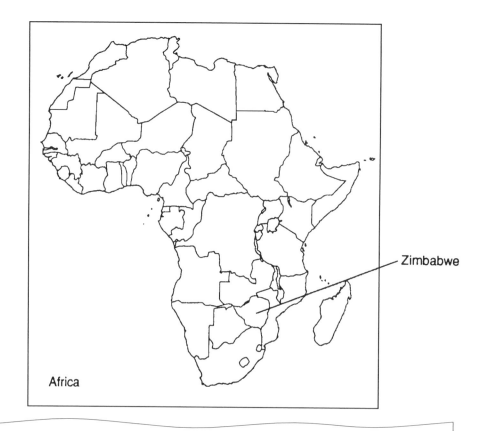

Zimbabwe

Africa

Your idea sounds very exciting. Yes, I do think you should apply to come to one of the English-speaking African countries, particularly Zimbabwe. You're always telling me how much you want to come here – well, now's your chance! Don't forget to mention your level of English, your computer skills and your connections with Zimbabwe.

I'm sure an experience like this would help you in your future career!

Do let me know what you decide.

Love

   Sheila

Now write:

(a) a **letter** to WPA, applying for a work placement (about 150 words)

(b) a **letter** to Sheila, telling her what you have done and asking for her advice (about 100 words).

You do not need to include addresses. You should use your own words as far as possible.

Part 2

Choose **one** of the following writing tasks. Your answer should follow exactly the instructions given. Write approximately 250 words.

2   You see the announcement below in *Society Worldwide*, an international magazine.

> **CHILDHOOD – PAST AND PRESENT**
>
> We invite you, our readers, to submit an article on family celebrations which you remember, to be included in our forthcoming series on the changing nature of childhood.
> Share your memories with our readers, describing some examples of celebrations from your own childhood **and** explaining clearly how such celebrations may be different for children today.

Write your **article**.

3   Most tourists who come to your country only visit the same few overcrowded places. Consequently the Tourist Board is trying to encourage people to spend holidays in the countryside, and it is planning a new brochure called *The Undiscovered Countryside*. You have been asked to write a contribution to the brochure. You should include information about what can be done on a countryside holiday, what kinds of accommodation are available and what the weather conditions are likely to be.

Write the **contribution to the brochure**.

4   You were contacted by an international research company and you agreed to help them with their investigation into the effect of television on young people. You then interviewed fifty people of various ages in your area, using the questions below.

> **INTERNATIONAL SURVEY ON TV AND THE UNDER-18s**
> • Are today's young people watching too much TV?
> • What influences – good or bad – does TV have on the young?
>
> Please submit your report to MRM TV Research, Channel Street, Edinburgh.

Write your **report**.

5   You are in the middle of a two-week residential training course with some colleagues from work; the course, the accommodation and some other facilities have provoked both positive and negative reactions from your colleagues. A senior colleague who was going to attend the course with you had to cancel at the last moment because of illness. You decide to write her a memorandum summarising your reactions and those of your colleagues.

Write the **memo**.

PAPER 3 ENGLISH IN USE (1 hour 30 minutes)

Part 1

For questions **1–15**, read the article below and then decide which word on page **43** best fits each space. Put the letter you choose for each question in the correct box on your answer sheet. The exercise begins with an example **(0)**.

Example:

0	A	0
		▭

THE TRADE IN RHINO HORN

Last year thieves broke into a Scottish castle and stole only one thing: a rhino horn, which at 1.5 metres was the longest in the world. In China pharmaceutical **(0)** ..... have been building up **(1)** ..... of antiques made from rhino horn, for the sole **(2)** ..... of smashing them to powder to make the **(3)** ..... ingredient of many of their medicines. And in Africa poachers continue to die in the **(4)** ..... for the black rhino.

Recently, conservationists met to **(5)** ..... a campaign to persuade countries where rhino horn is **(6)** ..... part of the traditional medicine to **(7)** ..... to substitutes. The biggest **(8)** ..... to the survival of the rhinoceros is the **(9)** ..... of certain countries to enforce a ban on domestic **(10)** ..... in rhino horn.

The rhino horn is included in many **(11)** ..... for disorders ranging from fevers to nosebleeds. Horn, like fingernails, is made of keratin and has no proven medicinal **(12)** ..... . Traditional substitutes, such as horn from buffalo or antelope, are **(13)** ..... as second best.

The battle is **(14)** ..... to be winnable. But it may be harder than the battle against the trade in ivory, for there is a **(15)** ..... between the two commodities. Ivory is a luxury; rhino horn, people believe, could save the life of their child.

0	(A)	factories	B	plants	C	workshops	D	studios
1	A	amounts	B	bundles	C	collections	D	groups
2	A	reason	B	intention	C	need	D	purpose
3	A	essential	B	real	C	actual	D	true
4	A	chance	B	search	C	fight	D	race
5	A	design	B	plan	C	programme	D	form
6	A	hardly	B	even	C	nearly	D	still
7	A	vary	B	switch	C	modify	D	adjust
8	A	threat	B	danger	C	disaster	D	menace
9	A	rejection	B	denial	C	refusal	D	protest
10	A	business	B	commerce	C	selling	D	trading
11	A	recipes	B	aids	C	remedies	D	doses
12	A	capacity	B	values	C	control	D	powers
13	A	regarded	B	valued	C	known	D	reputed
14	A	imagined	B	dreamed	C	thought	D	viewed
15	A	variation	B	difference	C	gap	D	comparison

Part 2

For questions **16–30**, complete the following article by writing the missing words in the correct box on the answer sheet. **Use only one word for each space**. The exercise begins with an example **(0)**.

Example:

0	by

	0

WRONGED BY HOW YOU WRITE

The handwriting of school children could spell the difference between success and failure in examinations according to research carried out by the Open University.

In a study **(0)** ..... Dennis Briggs of the Faculty of Educational Studies, it was found that essays which were written **(16)** ..... different styles of handwriting attracted different marks. 'The findings suggest that **(17)** ..... is a borderline zone within examination marking where **(18)** ..... an essay is written may be almost as important as what the essay is about,' said Mr Briggs. Five essays were double marked **(19)** ..... the second marker unaware of the marks of the first marker. The essay scripts for the second marker **(20)** ..... been copied out in three writing styles. Two of the styles were ones **(21)** ..... had been the subject of continual criticism at school.

(22) ..... the markers were practising teachers who **(23)** ..... told that the effectiveness of double marking was **(24)** ..... checked. The results showed that a 12-year old who can present an essay one way will do better, perhaps **(25)** ..... better, **(26)** ..... a friend who presents the **(27)** ..... standard in terms of content but who **(28)** ..... not or cannot make it look so attractive. The conclusion is that school children may not do as **(29)** ..... as perhaps they could **(30)** ..... their handwriting is untidy.

Part 3

In **most** lines of the following text, there is **either** a spelling **or** a punctuation error. For each numbered line **31–46**, write the correctly-spelled word or show the correct punctuation in the box on your answer sheet. **Some lines are correct**. Indicate these with a tick (✓) in the box. The exercise begins with three examples **(0)**, **(00)** and **(000)**.

Examples:

0	✓	0
00	its	0
000	California	0

0	Since 1941 Los Angeles has been obtaining about fifteen per
00	cent of it's water supply by draining streams that feed Lake Mono
000	in california. Now the city has been told to stop taking so much
31	water. Local environmentalist, Chris Moore explained that the
32	lake is an important habitat for millions of migratry birds and the
33	shrimps on which they feed. "Since the diversion of water began,"
34	he explained, "the level of the lake has droped more than ten
35	metres. This has created land bridges that make it easy for
36	predators to cross over to attack birds on island nesting sights."
37	A judge has ordered Los Angeles to limit the diversion of Lake
38	Mono water untill the lake can rise to an acceptable level. But
39	how will this be achieved The state has recently authorised the
40	expenditure off more than sixty million dollars to help pay for new
41	water sauces. However, to get the money the city must reach
42	agreement with local environmental groups on ways to preserve
43	the lake. Once agreement has been achieved work can begin on
44	establishing alternative supplies of water. We fully realise this
45	won't be easy, on acount of the extremely dry conditions in this
46	area, but I'm sure well find a way," says the optimistic Chris.

Part 4

For questions **47–61**, read the two texts on pages **46–47**. Use the words in the boxes to the right of the text, listed **47–61**, to form a word that fits in the same numbered space in the text. Write the new word in the correct box on your answer sheet. The exercise begins with an example **(0)**.

Example:

0	accessible	0

BOOK REVIEW

SLADE'S NEW FILM GUIDE

Everyone who watches films frequently thinks of something they would like to check (e.g. the name of a film star). To find information, it has sometimes been necessary to consult several volumes that are not very **(0)** ..... . This book aims to bring all the available sources together, while excluding out-of-date information and anything else that is considered **(47)** ..... . For most people a **(48)** ..... comprehensive work would be too weighty, but this condensed one should satisfy most **(49)** ..... . The contents are arranged **(50)** ..... , there is an **(51)** ..... on each film which seems important or influential, and there are notes on general subjects like censorship. Not **(52)** ..... , many readers will disagree with the selection and the assessments as any guide will inevitably be **(53)** ..... .

(0)	**ACCESS**
(47)	IMPORT
(48)	FULL
(49)	REQUIRE
(50)	ALPHABET
(51)	ENTER
(52)	SURPRISE
(53)	SUBJECT

ENCYCLOPAEDIA ENTRY

HOW WEATHER FORECASTS ARE DONE

Forecasting the likelihood of different types of weather coming in the near future can only be done with an understanding of what is happening **(54)** ..... . To acquire this, regular and accurate **(55)** ..... are needed, taken in different places to expose patterns of weather change. Weather **(56)** ..... have placed instruments all over the world, for the **(57)** ..... and transmission of **(58)** ..... data to weather stations. Many of these sites are staffed by meteorologists. However, in some sparsely **(59)** ..... or completely uninhabitable areas of the world, readings are often sent back by automatic equipment. For the **(60)** ..... of data, various instruments are used which can measure air-pressure, wind-speed, temperature and rainfall, and observations are made at least every day, in some cases **(61)** ..... .

(54)	CURRENT
(55)	MEASURE
(56)	SPECIAL
(57)	RECEIVE
(58)	PRECISION
(59)	POPULATION
(60)	COLLECT
(61)	HOUR

Part 5

For questions **62–74**, read the following informal note about a poetry competition and use the information in this text to complete the numbered gaps in the publicity leaflet about the competition. Then write the new words in the correct spaces on your answer sheet. **Use no more than two words** for each gap. The words you need **do not** occur in the informal note. The exercise begins with an example **(0)**.

Example:

0	annually	0
		— —

INFORMAL NOTE

Jack,

Believe it or not, it's been nearly a year since the last poetry competition and it's time to have it again this year. Can you put together a leaflet about it. Here are the points to include:

- We don't want poems to be longer than 30 lines.
- They can be written for either children or adults, but we want them to be entertaining, so explain that we'd really like ones that make people laugh.
- We can't afford to return poems, so if people want them back after the competition they'll have to send us a stamped, addressed envelope with the entry.
- People can send in as many entries as they like, but nobody will be able to win more than one prize.
- They've got to send an entry form in with their poem (they can get these from libraries and bookshops).
- We're charging £10 to enter the competition, and this should be sent with the entry form (but point out that they only pay £5 if they live in this area).
- Mention that entries must be in by March 27 and that the names of the people who will receive prizes will be known about a fortnight later.

PUBLICITY LEAFLET

CALLING ALL POETS!

A poetry competition is held in our town **(0)** ..... and entries are now being invited for this year's competition. Poems should be **(62)** ..... of thirty lines in length. They may be written with either children or adults **(63)** ..... , but this year the emphasis is on entertainment, and poems which display plenty of **(64)** ..... will be especially welcome. Unfortunately, because of the very **(65)** ..... of postage, entries will not be returned unless a stamped, addressed envelope **(66)** ..... with the entry. There is **(67)** ..... to the number of poems which may be submitted, but only one prize will **(68)** ..... to any one individual. Poems must be **(69)** ..... by an official entry form (obtainable from libraries and bookshops) together with the correct **(70)** ..... of £10. There is a **(71)** ..... rate available for **(72)** ..... residents. The **(73)** ..... is March 27 and the names of the prize-winners will be **(74)** ..... on April 10.

Part 6

For questions **75–80**, read the following text and then choose from the list **A–J** the best phrase given below to fill each of the spaces. Write one letter **(A–J)** in the correct box on your answer sheet. Each correct phrase may only be used once. **Some of the suggested answers do not fit at all.** The exercise begins with an example **(0)**.

Example:

0	J		0

NEW BUSINESS COURSES AT OXFORD AND CAMBRIDGE

Just a hundred years after the University of Pennsylvania established the world's first business school, Oxford and Cambridge, **(0)** ..... , are dipping their toes into the waters of management education. Recently, Cambridge University launched its first MBA (Masters of Business Administration) degree course, and Oxford University, **(75)** ..... , plans to open the doors of its own School of Management Studies soon. The two universities could not be entering the MBA arena at a worse time **(76)** ..... . Recession has halted recruitment in management consultancy and investment banking, **(77)** ..... . Those companies that are still hiring MBA graduates are cutting salaries **(78)** ..... . Many company directors complain that new MBA graduates are not as competent as they expected them to be, and say that they often need a considerable amount of in-company training. At the heart of the problem is the MBA curriculum, **(79)** ..... . Critics claim that a typical MBA course encourages a preference for theoretical knowledge rather than the insight that comes from practical experience. Many leading business schools are rethinking their courses **(80)** ..... . Only time will tell if these old universities can set new standards of excellence.

A but none has the luxury of Oxbridge's fresh start

·B which has changed little since the 1960s

·C because applications for such courses have fallen during the past two years

·D and that criticism has some force

·E and questioning what they are getting for their money

F because this re-training is increasingly important

G which are areas in which MBAs have been highly regarded and well-rewarded

H but conditions have changed radically since then

⅃ which is Cambridge's arch-rival in everything from astrophysics to rowing

J which are Britain's two most famous and prestigious universities

PAPER 4   LISTENING (45 minutes approximately)

Part 1

You will hear a phone-in service called, 'What's Happening This Month'. For questions **1–10**, look at the programme of events and fill in the information.

You will hear the recording **twice**.

LOCATION	EVENT	TITLE
International Studios	1	'People I have known'
2	Play	3
North Bank Theatre	4	5
6	Festival of World Conservation	7
Touring	Exhibition	8
Dartington Centre	9	10

Part 2

You will hear the representative of a travel company announcing changes to a holiday programme. For questions **11–16**, write down where the events and activities will now take place.

Listen very carefully as you will hear the recording ONCE only.

PROGRAMME

breakfast in: | | 11

morning excursion to: | | 12

shopping in: | | 13

lunch at: | | 14

afternoon: | | 15

dinner at: | | 16

Part 3

You will hear a radio programme about taking family photographs. For questions
17–24, complete the notes.

You will hear the recording **twice**.

These days, having one's photograph taken is less ⬚ **17**

One subject Gerald never photographs is ⬚ **18**

Photographic companies
want people to think that taking photos is ⬚ **19**

Ruth has put twenty pictures
on one page because she didn't like ⬚ **20**

When people see someone
taking pictures of them they tend to ⬚ **21**

Gerald says that family albums today do **not** show ⬚ **22**

According to Gerald, men are more interested
in recording family history when it involves ⬚ **23**

Women make history by ⬚ **24**

Part 4

You will hear five short extracts in which various people are talking about some aspect of travelling.

You will hear the recording **twice**. While you listen you must complete **both tasks**.

TASK ONE

For questions **25–29**, match the extracts as you hear them with the people listed **A–H**.

A airline pilot	
	25
B sales representative	
	26
C history teacher	
	27
D coach driver	
	28
E holiday courier	
	29
F taxi driver	
G restaurant owner	
H motorway police officer	

TASK TWO

For questions **30–34**, match the extracts as you hear them with the phrases listed **A–H** that best describe each speaker's comment.

A explaining something new	
	30
B expressing disappointment	
	31
C displaying anger	
	32
D demonstrating a skill	
	33
E making a complaint	
	34
F boasting about something	
G rejecting an offer	
H making a comparison	

(This test is also suitable for groups of three students; this only occurs as the last test of a session where a centre has an uneven number of candidates. It takes about 23 minutes.)

PAPER 5   SPEAKING (15 minutes)

There are two examiners. One (the Interlocutor) conducts the test, providing you with the necessary materials and explaining what you have to do. The other examiner (the Assessor) will be introduced to you, but then takes no further part in the interaction.

Part 1 (3 minutes for pairs of candidates, 5 minutes for groups of three)

The Interlocutor will first ask you and your partner(s) a few questions. You will then be asked to find out some information about each other, on topics such as hobbies, interests, career plans, etc.

Part 2 (4 minutes for pairs of candidates, 6 minutes for groups of three)

You will each be given the opportunity to talk for about a minute, and to comment briefly after your partners have spoken.

The Interlocutor gives you a set of photographs and asks you to talk about them for about one minute.

You will then be given another set of photographs to look at. One of your partners talks about these photographs for about one minute.

If a group of three students is being tested, the Interlocutor will give you all another two photographs to look at. The final student talks about these photographs for about a minute.

When you have all had your turn, the Interlocutor will ask you to look at each other's pictures again and answer another question, which relates to the photographs.

Part 3 (4 minutes for pairs of candidates, 6 minutes for groups of three)

In this part of the test you and your partner(s) will be asked to talk together. The Interlocutor will place a new set of pictures on the table in front of you. This stimulus provides the basis for a discussion. The Interlocutor will explain what you have to do.

Part 4 (4 minutes for pairs of candidates, 6 minutes for groups of three)

The Interlocutor will ask some further questions, which will lead to a more general discussion of what you have talked about in Part 3 and in which you will be encouraged to comment on what your partner(s) say(s).

Test 3

Paper 1 Reading (1 hour 15 minutes)

Part 1

Answer questions **1–16** by referring to the magazine article on page **57** in which various women are interviewed about their sports.

Indicate your answers **on the separate answer sheet.**

For questions **1–16** match the statements on the left below with the list of sportswomen **A–F** on page **57**.

Some choices may be required more than once.

She participates in a sport in which women are taking steps to gain equality with men.	**1**	**A** THE SKIER
She takes part in her sport on equal terms with men.	**2**	**B** THE CYCLIST
Her concentration at work is affected by her sporting activities.	**3**	**C** THE ROWER
She was surprised to discover her talent for her sport.	**4**	**D** THE LONG DISTANCE WALKER
She invests her earnings in her sport.	**5**	
It is considered strange for women to take part in her sport.	**6**	**E** THE SALOON CAR RACER
She spends less time on other activities than she used to.	**7**	**F** THE TRIATHLETE
The age at which women start her particular sport is significant.	**8**	
She was once under pressure to achieve her target by a certain date.	**9**	
She has a good income from her sport.	**10**	
She has endured physical suffering.	**11**	
It is difficult for women to get good training in her sport.	**12**	
She is sometimes afraid when taking part in her sport.	**13**	
She doesn't want her appearance to affect her sporting reputation.	**14**	
Her personality has changed since she started doing her sport.	**15**	
Women's achievements in her sport receive less publicity than men's.	**16**	

GREAT SPORTS
Women on a winning streak

To excel in any sport is hard enough, even for men, but women have to be twice as tough. Training and competition leave little time for a normal life, so sacrifices must be made. But against all the odds they are beating prejudice and breaking records. Here, we talk to just a few brilliant British sportswomen who are achieving their goals.

A   Jill, 27, skier
"It's a great feeling to fly through the air and land cleanly, but it can be scary. Sometimes you don't feel well or it's windy and you can't see, but you just get on with it. It's not easy to have a career outside skiing because we train for ten months of the year. You give up a lot of your social life and friends. But it was my choice. There are six men and three women in the British team. We all compete on the same courses at the same competitions and get treated the same — it's a young sport."

B   Caroline, 22, cyclist
"Two years ago I borrowed a bike to take part in a charity race. I won overall just because I cycled faster than everyone else, which was amazing because I'd never cycled before! I'm well paid as a pro, and cycling has lots of potential in terms of endorsements. However, I know I'm not ugly and it worries me that people may think I've got where I am because of how I look, not because I'm the best cyclist. So I tend to concentrate on the cycling at the moment, rather than earning money. I do at least four hours' training every day on the bike, plus some stretching exercises, swimming and running. My boyfriend's a cyclist as well, so he knows the time you have to put into it — it would be impossible otherwise."

C   Annabel, 26, rower
"Rowing is hard for girls to get into because very few girls' schools do it. So most don't start till they're 19 or 20 which makes it harder to succeed at an international level. Also, you usually have coaches who only stay a year or so. There's no continuity, so the women's squad is basically a shambles. But it's great fun and I love being fit, plus there's a good social life."

D   Ffyona, 24, long distance walker
"At 13 I dreamed of walking around the world — I didn't know just how big it was then! But Britain was too claustrophobic, too safe. I was very headstrong; I hated anyone having control over me. Now I am more tactful. Each walk has been different.

The walk across Australia was the worst experience I've ever had as far as pain is concerned. I was doing 50 miles and 21 hours each day with three hours' sleep in high temperatures and walking with 15 blisters on each foot. But I got the record! I had to, because my sponsorship money was going to run out after 95 days. Men think that women are more likely to fail, so sponsoring them is always seen as a higher risk."

E   Lisa, 26, saloon car racer
"Some men have huge egos when they're driving — you see it on motorways. When I'm doing well, they don't talk to me. Being a woman has its disadvantages.

When I get to a corner, the men think 'I've got to beat her', so I've had a lot of knocks!

You have to be naturally competitive and aggressive. It's very difficult to earn any money, and what I do make goes back into the sport. Women have been racing since the twenties and have always been classed as eccentrics. It's great that there are now more and more women taking up racing every year. For me, the appeal of saloon car racing is aiming for perfection — always trying to get round with a perfect lap."

F   Alison, 28, triathlete
"I get up at 5.30 three mornings a week to swim. I need Tuesday and Thursday mornings to catch up on my sleep. In the evening I just cycle or run. Yes, I do fall asleep at my desk sometimes! There is a lot of nervous build-up beforehand and when you're racing you really push yourself — you don't feel good if you don't. Several times I've asked myself why I do it. The answer is a) I'm happier when I keep fit, b) I'm a slob at heart and if I didn't make myself do this I'd really be one, c) racing is very social.

Men and women usually compete together but when an event is given coverage in the press, 90 per cent of the article will explain the men's event and 10 per cent will say, 'Oh, by the way, so-and-so won the women's event.' The prize money isn't as good either, of course. But now we've formed an International Triathlon Women's Commission, so we're working on it."

Part 2

For questions **17–23**, you must choose which of the paragraphs **A–H** on page **59** fit into the numbered gaps in the following newspaper article. There is one extra paragraph which does not fit into any of the gaps.

Indicate your answers **on the separate answer sheet**.

Sea, Ice & Rock

Mountaineer Chris Bonnington (58) is best known for scaling the summit of Everest in 1985. He has also pioneered routes in Britain and the Alps and written many books, including *Quest for Adventure* and *Everest the Hard Way*. Robin Knox-Johnston (53) began his sea career in the Merchant Navy.

In 1968–9 he was the first to circumnavigate the world single-handed, in his yacht *Sunhaili*. He broke the transatlantic record, taking 10 days to reach the Lizard from New York. The two teamed up to sail and climb in Greenland, recording the trip in their new book: *Sea, Ice and Rock*.

In 1979 I was working on *Quest for Adventure*, a study of post-war adventure. I called Robin to ask for an interview and he said would I like to join him for a sail. I could show him some climbing techniques and he could show me the rudiments of sailing.

17

The route was quite difficult and I was impressed at how steady Robin was in tricky conditions. He just padded quietly along. After a bit we arrived at this huge drop. I asked Robin if he had ever climbed before. He hadn't, so I showed him. When I had finished, Robin very politely asked if he could go down the way he climbed down ropes on his boat.

18

His proposal that we should combine our skills on a joint trip to Greenland was just an extension, on a rather grand scale, of our voyage to Skye. Robin impressed me immensely as a leader. Traditionally, the skipper makes all the decisions.

19

To be frank, I found the sailing trying and very boring. The moments of crisis which we had on the way back were easy to deal with: the adrenaline pumps and you get all worked up. The bit I found difficult was spending day after day in the middle of the sea.

20

To be honest, I felt a bit useless at times; I found that very trying. The crew was also packed very close together: six people on a 32ft yacht, designed to sleep four. At least when you're on a mountain expedition you have a chance to get away from each other.

21

Robin isn't a natural climber, which made his efforts even more impressive. The first time we tried to reach the pinnacle, we were on the go for 24 hours. On the way down we were dropping asleep on 50 degree slopes, 1,500 feet above the ground. Robin went to hell and back, but he totally put his confidence in me.

22

Yet he was all in favour of us having another go at climbing the mountain. The only time there was a near-crisis in our relationship was on the yacht on the way home. We were taking it in turns to be on watch. I was supposed to get up at 4 am for my shift, but Robin decided not to wake me. He felt he could do it himself.

23

While we enjoyed the Skye trip, we didn't really know each other until the end of the Greenland expedition. I found that underneath his bluff exterior, Robin was a kind-hearted, sensitive person.

A The previous night I'd almost dropped asleep. I felt that he didn't trust me – I felt insecure, and I said so. Robin immediately reassured me that I'd jumped to the wrong conclusion.

B But Robin made a point of consulting everyone first. Most of the time, nobody dared to advise him, but it was nice to feel you were part of the decision-making process.

C It was the first time I'd been on a yacht. We sailed for a while and then anchored. Robin's wife and daughter stayed on the boat and we paddled to the shore to exercise Robin's skills at climbing.

D When we reached Greenland and it was my turn to 'lead' the expedition, I found it difficult taking responsibility for Robin's life. There were many instances climbing together when if Robin had fallen, he could have pulled me off with him. I had to watch for that constantly. I underestimated how difficult the Cathedral – Greenland's highest mountain – would be.

E The winds were tricky and once again it was my turn to be on watch. I was aware that if I made a mistake I could take the mast out, which is horribly expensive and a real nuisance.

F He just followed. When it got too difficult and I realised we'd have to turn back, he accepted it. I also knew that Robin was worried about the boat: whether we'd be able to get it through the ice, whether it was in one piece.

G He was used to using his arms, I wanted him to use his legs. I wasn't too happy about it, but he lowered himself down quite safely. It was during that trip to Skye that Robin and I built the foundation of a very real friendship.

H I am a land-lover and not really a do-it-yourself type of person. Robin, in contrast, is a natural sailor and seemed to enjoy tinkering with the engine or mending the lavatory. I was aware that Robin didn't really need me.

Part 3

Read the following newspaper article and then answer questions **24–28** on page **61**. On your answer sheet, indicate the letter **A, B, C** or **D** against the number of each question **24–28**. Give only one answer to each question.

Indicate your answers **on the separate answer sheet**.

POWER DRESSING

EVERY SUMMER, the peacocks that roam free within Whipsnade Wild Animal Park in Bedfordshire expose their magnificent trains to the critical and often disdainful gaze of the hens. They re-enact the mystery that tormented Charles Darwin to his dying day: how in this competitive world, where nature – as Tennyson said – is red in tooth and claw, could birds have evolved such an obvious extravagance? How do they get away with it? The zoologist Marion Petrie and her colleagues of the Open University are now exploiting the quasi-wild conditions of Whipsnade to try, a century after Darwin's death, to settle the matter.

Darwin argued that living creatures came to be the way they are by evolution, rather than by special creation; and that the principal mechanism of evolution was natural selection. That is, in a crowded and hence competitive world, the individuals best suited to the circumstances – the 'fittest' – are the most likely to survive and have offspring.

But the implication is that fittest would generally mean toughest, swiftest, cleverest, most alert. The peacock's tail, by contrast, was at best a waste of space and in practice a severe encumbrance; and Darwin felt obliged to invoke what he felt was a *separate* mechanism of evolution, which he called 'sexual selection'. The driving mechanism was simply that females liked – in his words – 'beauty for beauty's sake'.

But Darwin's friend and collaborator, Alfred Russel Wallace, though in many ways more 'romantic' than Darwin, was in others even more Darwinian. 'Beauty for beauty's sake' he wanted nothing of. If peahens chose cocks with the showiest trains, he felt, then it must be that they knew what they were about. The cocks must have some other quality, which was not necessarily obvious to the human observer, but which the hens themselves could appreciate. According to Wallace, then, the train was not an end in itself, but an advertisement for some genuine contribution to survival.

Now, 100 years later, the wrangle is still unresolved, for the natural behaviour of peafowl is much harder to study than might be imagined. But 200 birds at Whipsnade, which live like wild birds yet are used to human beings, offer unique opportunities for study. Marion Petrie and her colleagues at Whipsnade have identified two main questions. First, is the premise correct – do peahens really choose the males with the showiest trains? And, secondly, do the peacocks with the showiest trains have some extra, genuinely advantageous quality, as Wallace supposed, or is it really all show, as Darwin felt?

In practice, the mature cocks display in groups at a number of sites around Whipsnade, and the hens judge one against the other. Long observation from hides, backed up by photographs, suggests that the hens really do like the showiest males. What seems to count is the number of eye-spots on the train, which is related to its length; the cocks with the most eye-spots do indeed attract the most mates.

But whether the males with the best trains are also 'better' in other ways remains to be pinned down. William Hamilton of Oxford University has put forward the hypothesis that showy male birds in general, of whatever species, are the most parasite-free; and that their plumage advertises their disease-free state. There is evidence that this is so in other birds. But Dr Petrie and her colleagues have not been able to assess the internal parasites in the Whipsnade peacocks to test this hypothesis. This year, however, she is comparing the *offspring* of cocks that have in the past proved attractive to hens with the offspring of cocks that hens find unattractive. Do the children of the attractive cocks grow faster? Are they more healthy? If so, then the females' choice will be seen to be utilitarian after all, just as Wallace predicted.

There is a final twist to this continuing story. The great mathematician and biologist R A Fisher in the thirties proposed what has become known as 'Fisher's Runaway'. Just suppose, for example, that for whatever reason – perhaps for a sound 'Wallacian' reason – a female first picks a male with a slightly better tail than the rest. The sons of that mating will inherit their father's tail, and the daughters will inherit their mother's predilection for long tails. This is how the runaway begins. Within each generation, the males with the longest tails will get most mates and leave most offspring; and the females' predilection for long tails will increase commensurately. Modern computer models show that such a feedback mechanism would alone be enough to produce a peacock's tail. Oddly, too, this would vindicate Darwin's apparently fanciful notion – once the process gets going, the females would indeed be selecting 'beauty for beauty's sake'.

24 What is the purpose of Marion Petrie's research?
   A to show that a peacock's train serves no useful purpose
   B to solve a problem that Charles Darwin could not solve
   C to compare peacocks in the wild with those in captivity
   D to demonstrate that Charles Darwin's theory was wrong

25 How did Alfred Russel Wallace's view of peacocks differ from that of Darwin?
   A He thought that a peahen's choice of mate was practical.
   B He believed that animals could experience emotions.
   C He believed animals appreciated beauty for its own sake.
   D He believed that the peacock's train must have a protective function.

26 Peahens at Whipsnade Zoo show a preference for
   A the most dominant male in a group.
   B the biggest and strongest male.
   C the male which displays most often.
   D the male with the finest feathers.

27 Why does Marion Petrie plan to study the offspring of different peacocks?
   A to check whether the birds have inherited diseases
   B to discover whether the breed is becoming bigger in general
   C to learn about the reasons behind the peahen's choice of mates
   D to study the development of various species

28 What does 'Fisher's Runaway' suggest?
   A that inherited characteristics gradually become stronger
   B that peacocks are exceptions to general biological laws
   C that peahens react instinctively to beauty
   D that Darwin underestimated the intelligence of animals

Part 4

Answer questions **29–43** by referring to the article about acupuncture on pages **63–64**.

Indicate your answers **on the separate answer sheet.**

For questions **29–43**, answer by choosing from paragraphs **A–H** on pages **63–64**. You may choose any of the paragraphs more than once.

Note: When more than one answer is required, these may be given **in any order**.

Which section(s) state that:

it is not easy to measure the effects of acupuncture scientifically?   29 ....   30 ....

the theory behind acupuncture is not entirely accepted by Western doctors?   31 ....   32 ....

acupuncture brings the body's own defences into operation?   33 ....   34 ....

accepted Western techniques can cause problems?   35 ....

needles may be inserted well away from the location of the pain?   36 ....

acupuncture patients may also be advised to visit a doctor?   37 ....

consideration of the patient's general state is important?   38 ....   39 ....

acupuncturists take into account the type of pain they are being asked to treat?   40 ....

not all acupuncture techniques are traditional?   41 ....

patients may try acupuncture because nothing else has worked? 42 ....

acupuncture does not hurt much?   43 ....

Ancient Chinese medicine in the West?

Acupuncture is two thousand years old. It comes from the traditional Chinese system of medicine that includes herbalism, massage, diet, manipulation and exercise. It is used to treat many different conditions, but acupuncture's role in treating pain has received most attention by doctors in the West. Some GPs, midwives and physios use it regularly for pain relief.

A   What's it all about?

Traditional Chinese medicine sees health as a state in which the energy of the mind, body and spirit are in harmony. According to the theory, energy or Qi (pronounced *chee*) flows around the body along lines called meridians. There are twelve main meridians, each linked to an internal organ, and lots of tiny meridians take Qi to every cell. When the flow of Qi is upset, blocked or weakened, the body is said to be out of balance: weakness or illness may result. During a consultation with a traditional acupuncturist, he or she will try to find where imbalances occur in the Qi. This is done by feeling pulses on your wrist, examining your tongue and assessing your general appearance. He or she will ask about your medical history, current health, general well-being, state of mind, and your eating and sleeping habits. An acupuncturist uses fine needles inserted into the skin. He or she may also apply warmth from smouldering herbs or pressure at points on meridians, to stimulate the flow of Qi.

B   Over three hundred points

The points used for acupuncture are related to meridians so won't necessarily be near the site of the complaint. People often say they feel a not unpleasant dull ache or tingling sensation when the needle is gently manipulated. This is either done by hand or by attaching the needle to an electro-acupuncture machine. Acupuncturists say this sensation shows the needle has reached the Qi in a meridian.

There are over three hundred points on the main meridians, with hundreds more elsewhere that are used less often.

C   Science tells us how

Without accepting the principles of traditional Chinese medicine, doctors here have accepted that acupuncture can work for pain relief. This is because they have been able to provide scientific explanations of how it might work. For example:

- It has been suggested that stimulating particular nerves blocks pain signals and stops them from reaching the brain.
- Some scientists believe that stimulating acupuncture points releases natural pain-relieving substances (endorphins).

D   What type of pain can be treated?

Many people with chronic long-term pain turn to acupuncture as a last resort. Back pain, sports injuries, arthritis, headaches and migraine and post-operative pain are commonly treated with acupuncture.

Other types of pain which acupuncturists claim to treat include menstrual pain, facial nerve pain and pain suffered by terminally ill people.

E   Modern use for an ancient treatment

Although acupuncture has been used in China for over 2,000 years, one development has been rather more recent. The use of acupuncture instead of anaesthesia during surgery only started in the 1950s. It was this that helped to convince some doctors outside China that there was more to acupuncture than mind over matter.

In China today, acupuncture is used during all sorts of operations, from tonsillectomies to caesareans, and is even used in open heart surgery. Needles may be used alone, with electrical stimulation or with drugs. It's claimed that the pain is more or less eliminated, but it varies from person to person. It's hard to imagine many of us finding the option of lying awake on the operating table very attractive. But acupuncturists say that acupuncture anaesthesia involves none of the side-effects of conventional anaesthetics (e.g. nausea), and you recover from it more quickly.

F Always effective

As with most complementary therapies, clinical trials to evaluate acupuncture are difficult to run. But trials that have been done have shown that 50 to 80 per cent of people find acupuncture effective for chronic pain. Acupuncturists generally quote a similar success rate. They accept that it won't work for everyone and that people vary in their responsiveness.
Traditional acupuncturists say that for chronic long-term pain it will usually take between six and seven visits for people to feel real relief. But some improvement should be felt after just two or three visits.

G A different approach to pain

But Western and Chinese medicine view pain rather differently. Like most alternative therapists, an acupuncturist views his or her patient in a holistic way. This means not just focusing on specific symptoms. An acupuncturist spends a long time making a diagnosis, trying to find underlying weaknesses in the Qi. He or she will also want to know what external factors are causing the pain. For instance, is the pain worse in the cold, heat, damp or wind? Does it feel sharp, dull, throbbing, constant or burning? These are seen as important factors in deciding how acupuncture can be used to treat the pain. It's unlikely that your average medical doctor would take such things into account, isn't it?

H Traditional or not?

Some medical professionals do have traditional acupuncture training. Others – including many GPs who practise acupuncture – reject traditional Chinese theory and subscribe to scientific explanations.
But many traditional acupuncturists believe that only by applying traditional Chinese medicine is it possible to bring about deep changes that lead to a longer cure – something that is very difficult to assess in trials.
Care should always be taken in choosing an acupuncturist, who should refer you to a medical doctor for further investigation if necessary.

PAPER 2   WRITING (2 hours)

Part 1

You **must** answer this question.

1   You have received a letter and a newspaper cutting from a teacher at the KPD School, where you attended an English course.

   Read the extract from the letter below and the newspaper cutting on page **66**. Then, using the information provided, write the **letter** and **note** listed on page **66**.

I'm sure you'll be interested in this article from the local paper of 11 September. It's terrible! They've made lots of mistakes – I've marked some of them. Mrs Driver has asked everybody to write to the paper to complain so that they have to print a correction – she's very worried that students will stop coming to the school. I thought I'd let you know. As an ex-student who had such a good time at KPD (and such excellent exam results!) you are just the right person to point out their mistakes. I hope you aren't too busy to help. If you do write to the paper, perhaps you would let Mrs Driver know too.

Take care and hope to see you soon.

   Andrea

Low standards at well-known school

Today 'Spotlight on Education' looks at the KPD School. This local school (Principal Mrs K. Driver) claims to offer excellent tuition but our investigation has shown that standards are in reality extremely low. Here are some examples of what we were told.

who by ?

Most teachers are lazy and don't prepare their lessons properly – perhaps that is the reason why students often leave the school knowing no more than when they started. And perhaps that is why very few students from this school ever pass any exams!

really ??!

you know that isn't true!

But quite apart from academic standards, there are other things wrong at KPD. Their brochure promises inexpensive social activities most afternoons and every weekend, but in the last six months there has been only one trip to another town – and that was too expensive for most students to afford. Speaking of price, the food served in the so-called 'restaurant' downstairs is incredibly expensive and the quality, like most other things at this school, is extremely poor.

No wonder everyone at KPD is so unhappy .....

no! at least one a month

special group rate

ridiculous!

Now write:

(a) a **letter** to the Editor of the paper, as requested by Andrea (about 200 words)

(b) a relevant **note** to Mrs Driver (about 50 words).

You do not need to include addresses. You should use your own words as far as possible.

Part 2

Choose **one** of the following writing tasks. Your answer should follow exactly the instructions given. Write approximately 250 words.

2   You have just seen the following advertisement on your college notice board:

COMPETITION

Help us to improve our English!

We need a better range of good magazines for the library and we want **you** to write a report on your **first** and **second** choices of magazines, telling us why you think they would benefit students.

Rules: 1.   **Magazines**, not books or newspapers.
              2.   Magazines in **English**.
              3.   **Real** magazines, not your own inventions!

Prize: A year's subscription to your own first choice of magazine.

Write your **report**.

3   Your college/workplace magazine has a regular feature about videos. This month it is your turn to select three currently available videos of different types (e.g. cinema film, pop/rock, educational, tourist, sports event) and write a **review** for the magazine, indicating why your colleagues, who are of varied nationalities, might or might not want to watch them.

4   It has become increasingly popular for students to spend a period of time studying in another country as part of their course. The *SIMON International Student Directory* contains information about educational systems throughout the world and aims to help students wishing to study abroad. You have been asked to write the entry about different types of educational opportunities in your country for students from the age of 16 upwards.

Write your **entry**.

5   As you are leaving your job in a multi-national company, you have been asked to write an article for the in-house magazine. Write about the job itself, the challenges of the job and the sort of person best suited to meet those challenges.

Write the **article.**

PAPER 3   ENGLISH IN USE (1 hour 30 minutes)

Part 1

For questions **1–15**, read the article below and then decide which word on page **69** best fits each space. Put the letter you choose for each question in the correct box on your answer sheet. The exercise begins with an example **(0)**.

Example:

0	B	0

THE NEW BRITISH LIBRARY

Originally commissioned 14 years ago, the new British Library was **(0)** ..... to open in 1990. However, the project has been **(1)** ..... by political infighting, poor planning and financial problems. The most recent **(2)** ..... came in June when inspectors discovered that 60 miles of new metal shelving had started to **(3)** ..... and needed to be **(4)** ..... . That would **(5)** ..... the opening of the project's first phase for yet another two years. ''Things have gone from bad to worse,'' said Brian Lake, secretary of the Regular Readers, an association of writers and scholars who are not happy with plans for the new library. ''It is a grand national project that has become a great national scandal.''

It sounded like a splendid idea when the government **(6)** ..... its £164 million project in 1978. Sophisticated electronic **(7)** ..... would help keep the library's irreplaceable stock at an optimal **(8)** ..... and humidity. A computer-controlled delivery system would provide books to readers within minutes of a **(9)** ..... rather than days. And to **(10)** ..... other needs of the reading public, the library would also include **(11)** ..... galleries, a restaurant and a conference hall.

That was the plan, **(12)** ..... . The start of construction was delayed until 1982 by arguments about planning and by a **(13)** ..... of government. Four years later, members of the cabinet ordered a **(14)** ..... report and discovered that the committee responsible for **(15)** ..... the project hadn't met in four years.

0	**A**	projected	**Ⓑ**	supposed	**C**	assumed	**D**	pretended
1	**A**	delayed	**B**	bothered	**C**	infected	**D**	restricted
2	**A**	comeback	**B**	setback	**C**	drawback	**D**	cutback
3	**A**	fade	**B**	melt	**C**	mould	**D**	rust
4	**A**	substituted	**B**	replaced	**C**	abandoned	**D**	rejected
5	**A**	distract	**B**	destroy	**C**	postpone	**D**	postdate
6	**A**	imposed	**B**	unveiled	**C**	claimed	**D**	manifested
7	**A**	items	**B**	computers	**C**	equipment	**D**	tools
8	**A**	heat	**B**	temperature	**C**	cold	**D**	warmth
9	**A**	reservation	**B**	demand	**C**	wish	**D**	request
10	**A**	fit	**B**	serve	**C**	bring	**D**	obey
11	**A**	exposition	**B**	show	**C**	exhibition	**D**	demonstration
12	**A**	especially	**B**	anyway	**C**	eventually	**D**	meanwhile
13	**A**	variation	**B**	difference	**C**	shift	**D**	change
14	**A**	progress	**B**	progression	**C**	progressive	**D**	progressing
15	**A**	guarding	**B**	supervising	**C**	overlooking	**D**	watching

Part 2

For questions **16–30**, complete the following article by writing the missing words in the correct box on the answer sheet. **Use only one word for each space.** The exercise begins with an example **(0)**.

Example:

0	so		0

CHANGING CITIES

What will the city of the future look like? This question has been asked **(0)** ..... many times over the past 500 years – and answered inconsequentially **(16)** ..... equal number of times – that we **(17)** ..... be sure of **(18)** ..... thing only: no one can predict with **(19)** ..... degree of accuracy how cities will look 50 or 500 years from now.

The reason is simple. Cities change continually. In the last fifty years they **(20)** ..... changed so rapidly that the oldest residents will remember a time **(21)** ..... their city seemed to belong not just to another era **(22)** ..... to a different dimension.

(23) ..... is true both of planned and unplanned cities. Planned cities such as New York and Paris, **(24)** ..... are closely organised on a grid or diagram of streets and avenues, have effectively burst at the seams this century, **(25)** ..... unplanned cities such as London, Tokyo and Los Angeles have grown just **(26)** ..... dramatically. Although their centres might remain much as they were many years **(27)** ..... , their suburbs have spread **(28)** ..... the tentacles of an octopus.

Some economists argue that expansion is a sign of a healthy economy **(29)** ..... that expanding cities are **(30)** ..... that attract international investment.

Part 3

In **most** lines of the following text, there is **either** a spelling **or** a punctuation error. For each numbered line **31–46**, write the correctly-spelled word or show the correct punctuation in the box on your answer sheet. **Some lines are correct**. Indicate these with a tick (✓) in the box. The exercise begins with three examples **(0)**, **(00)** and **(000)**.

Examples:

0	piece	0
00	it's	0
000	✓	0

WOOD

0	If we look at a peice of wood through a powerful microscope,
00	we can see that its made up of bundles of elongated cells
000	which closely resemble drinking straws. It is through these
31	cells that the nutrients from the soil and water travel, from
32	the routes of the tree, through the trunk, to the branches and
33	leafs. Their long shape makes them ideal for this purpose.
34	The trunk of the tree consists of the outer bark a layer of
35	young, light-coloured wood which is just under the bark, and
36	a central core of darker and harder wood. The name's for these
37	two types of wood are 'sapwood' and heartwood'. During
38	each years growing season, the tree adds a layer of wood
39	just inside the bark. As more sap rises, in the spring than at
40	any other time of year, this light-coloured wood is called 'spring
41	wood'. This type of wood has large, soft cells. In contrast the
42	wood which grows in summer is denser and darker in colour.
43	This differance in colour between spring and summer wood
44	is what produces the rings which we can see in the cross section
45	of a log. Counting these anual rings reveals the age of the tree.
46	Fast-growing trees produce wider rings and so there wood is softer.

Part 4

For questions **47–61**, read the two texts on pages **72–73**. Use the words in the boxes to the right of the text, listed **47–61**, to form a word that fits in the same numbered space in the text. Write the new word in the correct box on your answer sheet. The exercise begins with an example **(0)**.

Example:

0	growth	**0**

JOB ADVERTISEMENT

SALES EXECUTIVE

Due to the increasing **(0)** ..... of our operation both within the UK and abroad, we have **(47)** ..... for two recruiting **(48)** ..... . Our main focus of attention is within the telecommunications industry, but we would welcome **(49)** ..... from any good sales background, not necessarily within telecommunications. The ideal candidate will have **(50)** ..... sales experience, excellent communication skills, a **(51)** ..... to high service standards, a good sense of humour and an **(52)** ..... to be successful in a team context. We offer an attractive **(53)** ..... including good basic salary, performance-related bonus, a company car after a qualifying period, and permanent health insurance.

(0)	GROW
(47)	VACANT
(48)	CONSULT
(49)	APPLY
(50)	SUBSTANCE
(51)	COMMIT
(52)	EAGER
(53)	PACK

GUIDE BOOK ENTRY

DIEPPE – A FRENCH TOWN NOT TO MISS

Dieppe's **(54)** ..... to Paris makes this much-loved seaside resort an attraction for weekend holiday breaks in winter and summer alike. The **(55)** ..... new marina enables sea-goers to make a stopover in the heart of the town, which is right next to the fishing harbour. Within easy reach of Paris, it has been designated as a town of art and history. The **(56)** ..... white-brick buildings remind one that Dieppe was entirely **(57)** ..... after the great fire in 1649. The restoration of the town centre, **(58)** ..... respecting the original architecture, lends a special charm. The castle museum, **(59)** ..... the town, seemingly watches over its people. Its views across the valley are particularly **(60)** ..... . Dieppe has an intense cultural life and is the birthplace of 'Coast to Coast', a Franco-British meeting of choreographers and dancers. ''I can recommend without **(61)** ..... a visit to this wonderful town!''

(54) CLOSE
(55) SPECTACLE
(56) CHARACTER
(57) BUILD
(58) STYLISTIC
(59) DOMINATE
(60) IMPRESS
(61) HESITATE

Part 5

For questions **62–74**, read the formal letter about a meeting and use the information in it to complete the numbered gaps in the informal letter to the writer's friend. Then write the new words in the correct spaces on your answer sheet. **Use no more than two words for each gap**. The words you need **do not** occur in the formal letter. The exercise begins with an example **(0)**.

Example:

0	sorry	0

FORMAL LETTER

The Secretary
North of England Wildlife Protection Society
1 Hill Road
Burnley

Dear Mr Eagleton

Re: Annual General Meeting

I regret to inform you that I am unable to attend this meeting because a prior engagement will prevent me from arriving in time. Unfortunately, it is necessary for me to remain in Leeds on that evening as I have already agreed to participate in my younger brother's school-leaving ceremony. In fact, I have agreed to address the whole school on my work as a National Park manager. It might be possible for me to be at the meeting about half an hour before the time it is scheduled to finish, but I think that this would serve no purpose.

I have forwarded my report to Mrs Mary Jones, who I am hoping will kindly agree to read it to the meeting. Any questions can be directed to her and she will be able to answer them. I do not anticipate any problems, but if clarification is required, I can be contacted on my mobile phone during the evening.

I am confident that the meeting will be a great success.

Yours sincerely

Jack Robbins

INFORMAL LETTER

Dear Mary

I am **(0)** ..... to tell you that I can't **(62)** ..... to the annual meeting. There is **(63)** ..... that I have to go to on the same evening. There is just not enough time to do both. I can't **(64)** ..... Leeds on that evening because I have promised to **(65)** ..... in the school-leaving do at Bob's school – he's my younger brother, as you must remember. It's not just a matter of being there – I'm going to give **(66)** ..... , and, as you've probably guessed, it's about **(67)** ..... I do. I could get to Burnley just before **(68)** ..... of the meeting but it would be **(69)** ..... of time. I am **(70)** ..... my report with this letter. Could you do me **(71)** ..... and read it out at the meeting? Would you mind? I know that you can **(72)** ..... anything that comes up. I am sure there won't be any problems, but if there's anything people don't **(73)** ..... , you can give me **(74)** ..... . I'll keep the mobile switched on!

I hope everything goes well.

Best wishes

Jack

Part 6

For questions **75–80**, read the following text and then choose from the list **A–J** the best phrase given below to fill each of the spaces. Write one letter **(A–J)** in the correct box on your answer sheet. Each correct phrase may only be used once. **Some of the suggested answers do not fit at all.** The exercise begins with an example **(0)**.

Example:

```
0 | J                  0
                       ----
```

THE PROBLEMS OF TELEVISION NEWS

The trouble with television news bulletins is that not only will they never please all the people all the time, they'll probably annoy most of the people a lot of the time. In only half an hour they cover the globe **(0)** ..... .

All the words in one television bulletin would fit onto just the front page of one large newspaper. Yet viewers expect to see as much as there is in a whole newspaper. No one reads a newspaper from cover to cover: readers can flick through **(75)** ..... . On television, they have to sit through all the stories they don't want **(76)** ..... .

The typical news story contains a twenty-second introduction from the presenter, two twenty-second quotes from key people, forty seconds of commentary over pictures, **(77)** ..... . How much can you cram into that tight format **(78)** ..... ? Television is the hardest, most demanding kind of journalism there is.

Some viewers complain that bulletins should be longer **(79)** ..... . However, it appears that a mass audience will not watch for more than half an hour. And how much of the news do people really take in anyway? I doubt if anyone ever watches the news from start to finish, **(80)** ..... . There is no right answer, no perfect bulletin. Large numbers of viewers will always complain.

A and be an important educational influence

B and concentrates all the way through

C and may be disappointed if their particular interest isn't featured

D and still make sense

E and they can hardly remember what they have seen

F and go into much more detail

G and reach a much wider audience

H and find the item they want

I and then a reporter summing everything up

J and struggle to do the impossible

PAPER 4   LISTENING (45 minutes approximately)

Part 1

You will hear a travel company's information line recording giving details of its holidays in Crete. For questions **1–8**, fill in the information.

You will hear the recording **twice**.

When you fly to Crete from the UK you [____ **1**] change planes.

There are flights [____ **2**] a week from three UK airports.

If you need to take [____ **3**] , you have to make a contribution towards the extra cost.

The tyres and windscreen of a hired car are [____ **4**]

Weekly car hire ranges from £ [to £ ____ **5**]

You won't have to [____ **6**] in most properties.

In some resorts you don't have to pay for [____ **7**]

Senior citizens pay [____ **8**] than the normal holiday cost.

Part 2

You are on a tour of England and your coach has just arrived in Fancaster. The courier is telling you the history of the town before you explore it. For questions **9–17**, complete the notes about the town.

Listen very carefully as you will hear the recording ONCE only.

FANCASTER

2500–2250 BC: _____ **9**

1st century AD: Romans arrived, used Fancaster as

_____ and _____ **10**

Only trace of Romans:

_____ **11**

5th century AD: _____ **12**

12th century AD: increase in _____ **13**

1287:   town _____ **14**

About 1320:   started _____ **15**

1340s: _____ **16**

Nowadays: _____ **17**

Part 3

Your will hear a radio interview with a university lecturer who was carrying out some research in a third world country when a flood disaster struck. For questions **18–27**, complete the notes.

You will hear the recording **twice**.

Her area of research: |_____ **18**|

People helping her: |_____ and _____ **19**|

Her feelings at not going to the provinces: |_____ **20**|

How she moved around in the floods: |_____ **21**|

A major source of danger: |_____ **22**|

Her feelings towards the poor: |_____ **23**|

Her feelings towards the merchants: |_____ **24**|

People who tried to help the poor: |_____ **25**| and

|_____ **26**|

Her feelings as the plane took off: |_____ **27**|

Part 4

You will hear various people talking about education.

You will hear the recording **twice**. While you listen you must complete **both tasks**.

TASK ONE

For questions **28–32**, match the extracts as you hear them with the people listed **A–H**.

A	politician	
B	employer	28
C	primary school teacher	29
D	parent	
E	sports coach	30
F	university professor	31
G	museum guide	
H	student	32

TASK TWO

For questions **33–37**, match the extracts as you hear them with each speaker's intention listed **A–H**.

A	asking advice	33
B	complaining	
C	ordering	34
D	offering	35
E	apologising	
F	describing part of a job	36
G	describing a procedure	
H	outlining a plan	37

PAPER 5   SPEAKING (15 minutes)

There are two examiners. One (the Interlocutor) conducts the test, providing you with the necessary materials and explaining what you have to do. The other examiner (the Assessor) will be introduced to you, but then takes no further part in the interaction.

Part 1 (3 minutes)

The Interlocutor will first ask you and your partner a few questions. You will then be asked to find out some information about each other, on topics such as hobbies, interests, career plans, etc.

Part 2 (4 minutes)

You will each be given the opportunity to talk for about a minute, and to comment briefly after your partner has spoken.

   The Interlocutor gives you a set of photographs and asks you to talk about them for about one minute. Each set of photographs has a different focus, so it is important to listen carefully to the Interlocutor's instructions. The Interlocutor then asks your partner a question about your photographs and your partner responds briefly.

   You will then be given another set of photographs to look at. Your partner talks about these photographs for about one minute. This time the Interlocutor asks you a question about your partner's photographs and you respond briefly.

Part 3 (4 minutes)

In this part of the test you and your partner will be asked to talk together. The Interlocutor will place a new set of pictures on the table between you. This stimulus provides the basis for a discussion. The Interlocutor will explain what you have to do.

Part 4 (4 minutes)

The Interlocutor will ask some further questions, which will lead to a more general discussion of what you have talked about in Part 3 and in which you will be encouraged to comment on what your partner says.

Test 4

Paper 1   Reading (1 hour 15 minutes)

Part 1

Answer questions **1–13** by referring to the reviews of crime novels on page **83**.

Indicate your answers **on the separate answer sheet.**

For questions **1–13** match each of the statements below **(1–13)** with one of the novels **(A–H)** reviewed on page **83**.

Some choices may be required more than once.

It takes place in a poor district.	1 ....
The main character is not typical of this kind of novel.	2 ....
The main character is feeling dissatisfied with his current work.	3 ....
It has a particularly dramatic opening.	4 ....
The main character remains determined despite opposition.	5 ....
The reader feels sure that the main character will solve the crime.	6 ....
It features people's peculiarities.	7 ....
It is likely to amuse you.	8 ....
It is too long.	9 ....
It successfully combines the conventional elements of this kind of novel.	10 ....
It is not as good as the writer's other books.	11 ....
It is impossible to predict the ending.	12 ....
The suspense is particularly skilfully managed.	13 ....

BOOK A

Steve Martin's **Compelling Evidence** is compelling indeed. The narrator, a lawyer struggling to build a new practice after being forced to leave a high-powered law firm, finds himself manoeuvred into defending his boss's wife when she is tried for her husband's murder. The trial scenes are riveting, with the outcome in doubt right up to the verdict, and a really unexpected twist in the final pages. This is a terrific debut into a crowded genre.

BOOK B

Curtains for the Cardinal begins with a bang, and plunges the charismatic Sigismondo, troubleshooter for the aristocracy of the Italian Renaissance, into a turmoil of politics, clerical intrigue and high-society murder from which we are always confident he will emerge unscathed to disclose the guilty parties. The plot is convoluted and the book is about 50 pages overweight, but it is still great stuff.

BOOK C

File Under: Deceased introduces a refreshingly different new detective from a first novelist, Sarah Lacey. Leah Hunter is a tax inspector, ideally positioned, it seems, for a bit of investigating when a strange man falls dead at her feet. Undaunted by attacks from various quarters – perhaps tax inspectors are used to this sort of thing – and the disapproval of her handsome local detective sergeant, gutsy, versatile Leah is a winner in every way.

BOOK D

Double Deuce by Robert B. Parker sets that most literate of private investigators, Spenser, the job of assisting his friend Hawk to clear drug dealers out of a deprived estate in rundown Boston. The slick dialogue comes almost as fast as the bullets, but there are few corpses and more philosophy than usual. High-quality entertainment, as always from Parker.

BOOK E

False Prophet by Faye Kellermann, features her usual pair of detectives, Pete Decker and Marge Dunn, investigating an attack and burglary at the house of a legendary film star's daughter. The author's easy writing style and eye for odd human behaviour make this an entertaining mystery.

BOOK F

Husband and wife, Diane Henry and Nicholas Horrock, write as a team. **Blood Red, Snow White** features another lawyer, another female client, but the action is all outside the courtroom and the defender finds himself becoming the victim as the plot unravels. All the classic ingredients of romance, money and violence are mixed efficiently to produce an engrossing suspense novel.

BOOK G

Dead for a Ducat by Simon Shaw presents actor Philip Fletcher in a new role, that of intended victim. The hilarious collection of characters are brought together to film the story of *Robin Hood*, but Philip isn't the only person to feel this is not the way his career should be developing. Simon Shaw never fails to entertain, but in moving his star actor from black comedy to farce, he gives a performance below his usual high standard.

BOOK H

Fall Down Easy is Lawrence Gough's best book for some time. Canadian police hunt a versatile bank robber who preys on female bank tellers. The slow, expertly-paced build-up of tension and the portrayal of the clever, disturbed robber raise this way above the average detective novel.

Part 2

For questions **14–20**, you must choose which of the paragraphs **A–H** on page **85** fit into the numbered gaps in the following magazine article. There is one extra paragraph which does not fit in any of the gaps.

Indicate your answers **on the separate answer sheet**.

THE LONG-DISTANCE RUNNER

Richard Nerurkar, one of Britain's top 10,000-metre runners, visits the Kenyans' high-altitude training camp.

Ten miles south of the equator, a stony mountain track leads off the quiet metalled road from Nairobi. The track marks the start of the trek up Kenya's highest peak, the glacier-capped Mount Kenya. This gorgeous, if lonely and isolated, spot is Nanyuk: for the past three years it has been my base for mid-winter altitude training in Kenya's Central Highlands.

14

I was invited by Kenya's national team coach when I finished fifth – behind three Kenyans and a Moroccan – in the World Championship 10,000 metres race. It was an opportunity not to be missed. Training at high altitude produces more red blood cells, which improves oxygen-carrying capacity.

15

My first African race – which came before my spell at the Kenyan team training camp – was also a first for the whole continent. Held in Nairobi, it was the first-ever international cross-country race to be held on African soil.

16

However, I don't believe Kenyan success can entirely be put down to the altitude factor. Kenyan runners are also noted for their refreshingly uncomplicated approach to the sport. While their running style is seemingly effortless, their diet simple and their manner of conversation relaxed, they also seem to love competing.

17

The national team training camp is at St Mark's College, 6,200 feet up the southern slope of Mt Kenya, surrounded by beautiful playing fields and dense tropical vegetation.

18

The athletes' days at the camp are dominated by three work-outs: a leisurely early-morning run, interval training at mid-morning, followed by a steady run in the late afternoon. The daily regime began at six. We crawled from our bunks and assembled to be briefed by the coaches for the morning run.

"Run easy, you have a hard job today", we were warned as we left by the coach who'd invited me.

The total distance covered each day was about 40 kilometres – a little short of a marathon distance. The only exception was Sunday, with just the one scheduled run of 20 kilometres, which certainly came as a welcome respite from the rest of the week's three daily work-outs.

19

Lunch and dinner both had a similar menu: ugali (a maize dish), stew, cabbage or spinach and tea. When the day's running was over, in the early evening, we would pile into a car and drive down to bathe properly in one of the many streams that run off from Mt Kenya's shrinking glaciers.

20

I couldn't stop myself pondering upon a rather different explanation: that the purity and simplicity of this mountainside lifestyle, these gruelling work-outs and this passion for success, perhaps these are the secrets, perhaps these are the real reasons behind Kenya's rise to the top of world distance running.

A But the least discussed aspect of the puzzle of Kenyan success was perhaps the most basic: how do they train? My stay with the Kenyan runners at their team training camp soon provided the answers.

B With smoke rising from huts in the valley to obstruct our view of the lush, green, tropical vegetation and deep chasms, the senior members of the team controlled the pace.

C These benefits have been borne out by the successes of generations of Kenyan runners.

D Running apart, life was complication-free. A splash of water on the face and a brush of the teeth sufficed for pre-breakfast preparations. Breakfast itself consisted of tea, bread and boiled eggs, taken in a sparsely-lit, small dining area.

E But not once on those trips had I trained with Kenyan runners on their home soil. On my fourth and most recent winter training trip to Kenya, however, I broke a personal tradition. I both competed in my first-ever race in Kenya's oxygen-thin air and stayed at Kenya's national team training camp, which is where the country's top runners prepare for their annual assault on the World Cross-Country Team Championships.

F If nothing else, it was a humbling experience. Of the 41 runners who finished ahead of me, all but 3 were Kenyan. And I honestly felt I hadn't had a bad race!

G By the time I left the camp, I was even more appreciative of Kenyan success. That success just can't be attributed to genetics or upbringing or altitude alone.

H It's a fairly basic affair, though: there are few comforts. The athletes live among the college's regular students and are housed six to a room in cinder-block dormitories.

Part 3

Read the following introduction from a book and then answer questions **21–25** on page **87**. On your answer sheet, indicate the letter **A, B, C** or **D** against the number of each question **21–25**. Give only one answer to each question.

Indicate your answers **on the separate answer sheet**.

ECCENTRICS

An eccentric is by definition someone whose behaviour is abnormal, someone who refuses to conform to the accepted norms of his society. This, of course, immediately begs the question, "What is normal?" Most of us, after all, have our quirks and oddities. It may be a passion for entering newspaper competitions, a compulsion for collecting beer mats, a tendency to write indignant letters to the press on every conceivable subject. Eccentricity is the assertion of our individuality. Within most of us that urge is constantly in conflict with the contrary force. It is as though in the depths of our psyche we have two locomotives head-to-head on the same track, pushing against each other. One is called individualism and the other conformity and in most of us it is conformity that is the more powerful. The desire to be accepted, loved, appreciated, to feel at one with our fellows, is stronger than the desire to stand out in the crowd, to be our own man, to do our own thing.

Notice, for example, how people who have unusual hobbies, strong opinions, or unconventional behaviour, tend to congregate. They form clubs, hold meetings, and organise rallies where they can get together and discuss their common enthusiasms or problems. The important word is 'common'. They look for other people with whom they can share what in the normal run of events is regarded by relatives, friends and neighbours as an oddity. A crowd, even a small crowd, is reassuring.

Probably all of us recognise a tension within ourselves between the two forces of individualism and conformity, for at the same time that most of us are going with the crowd, we tend to resent any suggestion that this is what we are doing. We feel a self-conscious need to assert our individuality as when the belligerent man at the bar informs his small audience, "Well, I say what I think." Or the wary stranger to whom we have just been introduced announces, "You must take me as you find me. I don't stand on ceremony."

Any of us can, at any time, reverse this trend. We can stoke the boiler of individualism, assert our own personality. Many people have made it to the top in their chosen professions, basically by doing just that. One example is Bob Dylan, the American singer, who has gone on record as saying, "When you feel in your gut what you are doing and then dynamically pursue it – don't back down and don't give up – then you're going to mystify a lot of folk." But that self-conscious assertion of individuality is not eccentricity, at least not in the early stages. When a pop singer deliberately wears bizarre clothes to gain publicity, or a society hostess makes outrageous comments about her guests in order to get herself noticed in the gossip columns, that is not eccentricity. However, if the pop star and the society hostess perpetuate such activities until they become a part of themselves, until they are no longer able to return to what most of us consider 'normal behaviour', then they certainly would qualify. For the most important ingredient of eccentricity is its naturalness. Eccentrics are not people who deliberately try to be odd, they simply *are* odd.

The true eccentric is not merely indifferent to public opinion, he is scarcely conscious at all. He simply does what he does, because of who he is. And this marks the eccentric as essentially different from, for example, enthusiasts, practical jokers, brilliant criminals, exhibitionists and recluses. These people are all very conscious of the world around them. Much of what they do, they do in reaction to the world in which they live. Some wish to make an impression on society, some wish to escape from society, but all are very much aware of society. The eccentric alone goes on his merry way regardless.

21 According to the writer, eccentric people
  A   want to show that they are different.
  B   try to do what is expected of them.
  C   express their own views in public.
  D   pretend to be something they are not.

22 Eccentric people tend to form into groups because
  A   they have no other friends.
  B   they want others to share their interests.
  C   they are good organisers.
  D   they feel they are misunderstood.

23 According to the writer, most people have a desire to
  A   be regarded as individuals.
  B   behave differently from other people.
  C   say what other people want to hear.
  D   spend all their time with a group of people.

24 In the writer's view, people who qualify as eccentrics
  A   make every effort to appear strange.
  B   have a strong desire to be noticed.
  C   deliberately behave in a mysterious way.
  D   are unaware that their behaviour is unusual.

25 What is the purpose of the article?
  A   to criticise people who always conform
  B   to encourage people to be individuals
  C   to examine the reasons for eccentric behaviour
  D   to describe problems faced by eccentric people

Part 4

Answer questions **26–42** by referring to the extract from a book about photography on pages **89–90**.

Indicate your answers **on the separate answer sheet**.

For questions **26–42**, answer by choosing from paragraphs **A–J** on pages **89–90**. You may choose any of the paragraphs more than once.

Note: When more than one answer is required, these may be given **in any order**.

Which paragraph emphasises the value of

asking the subject to look at something else in the picture?   **26** ....

including things which tell us more about the subject?   **27** ....

depicting human communication within a picture?   **28** ....

ensuring that everyone is clearly visible?   **29** ....

Which paragraph or paragraphs suggest that

people involved in activities make for good photographs?   **30** .... **31** ....

the look on the subject's face is the most influential element in a photograph?   **32** .... **33** ....

not everyone is comfortable in front of the camera?   **34** .... **35** .... **36** ....

you might try to make your subject respond naturally to something you do?   **37** ....

not only cheerful people make good pictures?   **38** ....

people may react negatively to being photographed?   **39** ....

you should suit your technique to the purpose of your photograph?   **40** ....

it can be a good idea to take a picture from above your subject?   **41** .... **42** ....

Photographing People

People are the most interesting of all subjects. A photograph with someone in it is almost always more compelling than the same shot without the human interest. People are also the most difficult subjects to photograph well. Apart from the technical and artistic considerations, the photographer has to be conscious of actions, gestures and expressions. And often the presence of the camera itself can have a disastrous effect on these.

A   GROUPING PEOPLE

Avoid straight lines in group shots. Ask people to stand at different angles and distances and if possible on different levels. Otherwise, have some of the group sitting or kneeling at the front so that you can see all the faces, or raise your own viewpoint.

B   POSING FOR PICTURES

People seldom act naturally in front of the camera. Often they stiffen up and the pose becomes rather wooden. Relax your subject by helping him to find a comfortable position. You might suggest he folds his hands or puts them in his pockets.

C   THE RIGHT APPROACH

Never try to pretend that you are not taking a picture of someone when it is clear that you are as this only creates tension and even hostility. Most people will agree to have their picture taken – perhaps after some initial protestations – and are quite flattered by it. But they are likely to become rather self-conscious and you may need to direct them. A picture can be spoiled by the fact that the subject is looking rather aimlessly out of the picture so that the interest lies elsewhere.

D   EYE CONTACT

A picture gains immediate impact if the subject appears to be looking at the viewer of the picture. Ask your subject to look into the lens – not necessarily to smile as well – and this is the effect you will get. The subject may not be able to do this for too long: he may become self-conscious or be distracted by someone nearby. So remind him once more, just before you release the shutter. Or try saying something funny or unexpected as you take the shot for a genuine reaction rather than a meaningless stare.

E   CANDID CONCENTRATION

An alternative to direct eye contact is for the subject to concentrate on something within the picture area. Your subject might find this easier to do, and the viewer can follow the attention to another part of the picture. You get the impression that you are observing the subject unnoticed. Candid shots have a special fascination and the subject's expression is vital to the picture.

F   EXPRESSIONS AND GESTURES

Expressions and the gestures that go with them tell us more about the subject of a photograph than anything else. Even if he is obviously badly treated and hungry, a laughing child provokes a smile from the viewer, whereas a sad expression produces a sympathetic sadness in the viewer, however apparently comfortable the subject may be. Look for familiar expressions for your portraits: shrugs, winks, anger, tears, thumbs-up, fist-clenching and so on. They are an instant visual language.

G   SITUATION INTEREST

Though shots which isolate a figure or face prominently have great impact, the subject's background or environment can add extra interest and information about the subject. When using a background in this way, try to exclude details that are not relevant to the subject or blur them by focusing selectively. Make sure that the subject is not overwhelmed by the background – a wide-angle lens will make your subject appear relatively larger by comparison with the background.

H   INTERACTION

Wherever two or more people are talking, arguing, haggling, joking or working together, there are opportunities for good pictures. Couples make appealing shots; so do mothers and babies, teachers and children or teams of people working or playing a sport. Look out especially for contact between the subjects – either eye-contact or physical contact, like a protective hand on the arm or a handshake. Or show how one is reacting to another by waiting for an animated expression or telling gesture.

I   PEOPLE AND PLACES

Many pictures of people are taken on holiday or during an outing – partly to show the place they were visiting. A little care will greatly improve this type of picture. To show people against a relevant background, use a standard or a wide-angle lens and move far enough back to get the whole building (or mountain, or lake) in the frame. Ask your subjects to come fairly close to the camera and compose the picture so that the group forms a foreground interest without obscuring the background. If you can find a slightly elevated camera position, this will be far easier to do. A good picture will show a balance between the subjects and the place they were visiting, so that both claim an equal share of the viewer's attention.

J   TO POSE OR NOT TO POSE?

In answer to this question, first decide why you want to take the picture. If you are taking a picture to remember someone by – someone you may have met briefly on holiday, for example – then you will want a good clear picture and it would be worth asking the subject to pose against a well-chosen background. Pictures of the family, on the other hand, can be very tedious if they are a succession of formal poses in front of places of interest. Candid pictures of events as they happen are far more lively, and you are more likely to get unselfconscious shots when you know the subject well. A picture taken on the spur of the moment will jog the family memory in future years far better than a posed portrait.

Visual materials for Paper 5

The Cunard White Star Liner "Queen Mary"

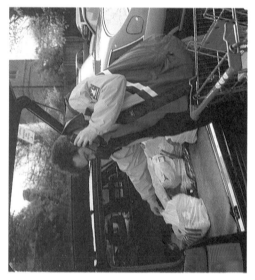

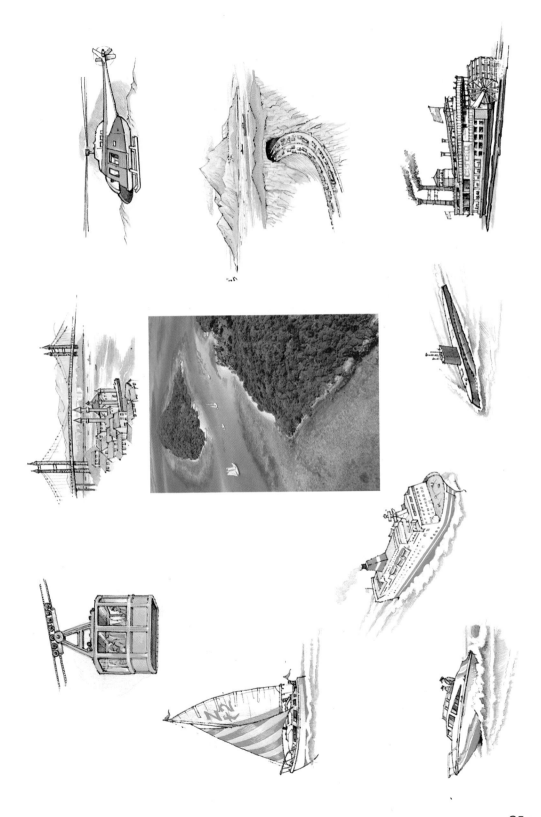

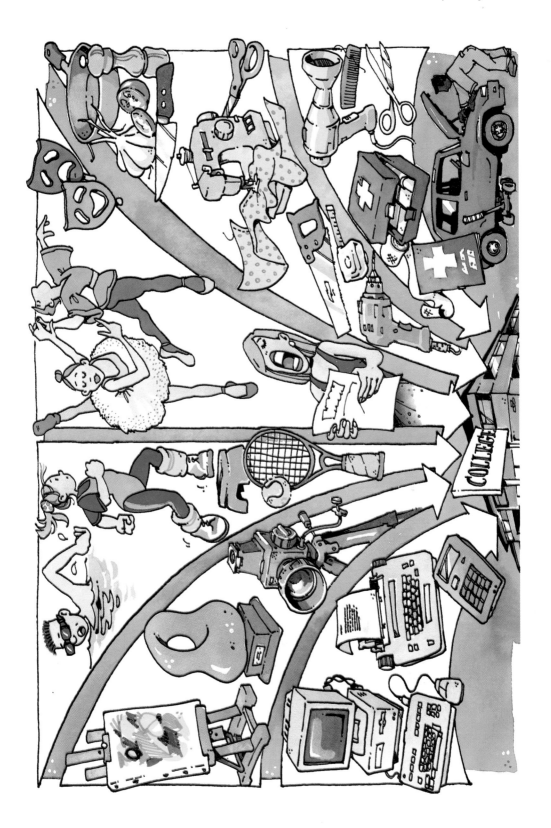

PAPER 2 WRITING (2 hours)

Part 1

You **must** answer this question.

1 A few months ago you joined an international friendship club which organises regular meetings in your town. You soon realised that although there is a friendly atmosphere, the meetings are rather dull. You have talked to other members who agree that some changes should be made and you have volunteered to write to the chairperson of the committee, Ms Jane Dennis.

Below is the club's next programme and the notes you made after talking to the members.

Read the programme and the notice on pages **91** and **92**. Then using the information provided write **the letter** outlined on page **92**.

THE INTERNATIONAL CIRCLE
THE CLUB FOR EVERYONE!

September programme

Sept 1   *New members' meeting – come and welcome new arrivals*
              Coffee and soft drinks in the clubroom 8 – 9pm

Sept 15   *"A travelling life"*
              Talk with slides by Carlo Maragna, retired teacher, about the countries he has visited during his long career.
              Clubroom 6 – 9pm

Sept 29   *Musical evening*
              Songs from around the world, led by Susanna Woodall at the piano.
              All your old favourites! Clubroom 7.30pm

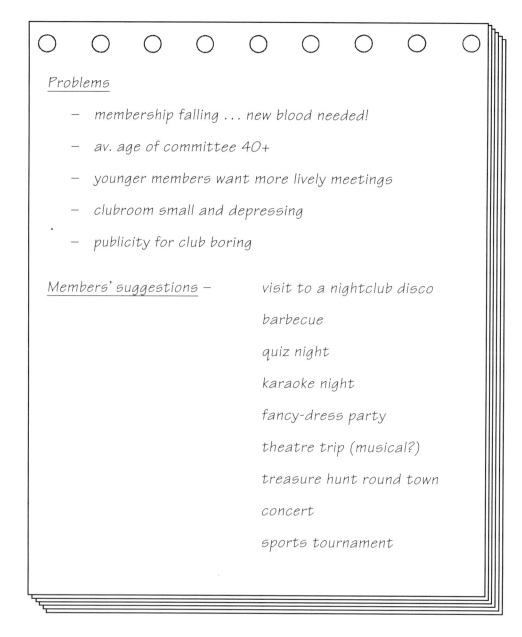

Problems

    — *membership falling ... new blood needed!*

    — *av. age of committee 40+*

    — *younger members want more lively meetings*

    — *clubroom small and depressing*

    — *publicity for club boring*

Members' suggestions —   *visit to a nightclub disco*

                             barbecue

                             quiz night

                             karaoke night

                             fancy-dress party

                             theatre trip (musical?)

                             treasure hunt round town

                             concert

                             sports tournament

Now write your **letter** to Ms Dennis explaining why it is felt that some changes would be a good idea. Make two or three suggestions for some rather different activities for future programmes and indicate why they would be successful (about 250 words).

Your do not need to include addresses. You should use your own words as far as possible.

Part 2

Choose **one** of the following writing tasks. Your answer should follow exactly the instructions given. Write approximately 250 words.

2   There has recently been a strike in your country which has affected some aspect of everyday life (e.g. transport, electrical/gas power, medical services, rubbish collection). Having heard exaggerated reports about it on TV, a friend abroad has written to you expressing his/her concern. Write a **letter** to reassure him or her, describing what has happened and how people are coping.

3   You have seen the following in an international magazine.

WANT A FREE TRIP TO YOUR IDEAL DESTINATION?

Tell us about recent improvements in facilities for visitors to your country. We'll publish the most informative articles each month and after six months we'll fly the author of the best article anywhere in the world.

HAVE THE HOLIDAY OF A LIFETIME!

Write the **article** about facilities for visitors to your country.

4   A new satellite TV series is being shown in your country. It seems worth watching for several reasons, including the quality of the English language used. Write a **review** of the series for your workplace/college newsletter, encouraging colleagues to watch regularly.

5   An international organisation is conducting research into employment prospects in different parts of the world. You have been asked to contribute a **report** entitled *Opportunities for School leavers* with particular reference to your local area. You should include information on kinds of employment available for young people, pay and conditions, and training possibilities.

PAPER 3   ENGLISH IN USE (1 hour 30 minutes)

Part 1

For questions **1–15**, read the article below and then decide which word on page **95** best fits each space. Put the letter you choose for each question in the correct box on your answer sheet. The exercise begins with an example **(0)**.

Example:

0	B		0

THEME HOLIDAYS IN SCOTLAND

If you like to build your holiday round a theme or particular **(0)** ..... , there are many opportunities open to you. The Scottish Tourist Board publishes an excellent **(1)** ..... , *Adventure and Special Interest Holidays in Scotland*, containing **(2)** ..... of dozens of ideas for 'different' holidays together with addresses to **(3)** ..... . Write for a copy to any of their offices.

   You can, for example, go on an archaeological holiday and be **(4)** ..... to the many prehistoric **(5)** ..... on the Solway Coast and the Early Christian remains at Whithorn. For creative people, there are any number of arts and crafts **(6)** ..... that offer instruction as well as **(7)** ..... . Prices vary, depending on the **(8)** ..... of teaching and accommodation. Subjects range from painting and music to wood-carving, silver-smithing and **(9)** ..... . Outdoor **(10)** ..... can choose from a wide range too – from bird watching to camping, from gliding to golf.

   If you've always wanted to see the west **(11)** ..... of Scotland from the sea but haven't got your own boat and prefer an experienced hand at the helm, try STA Schooners. They **(12)** ..... week-long voyages in the *Tall Ship Malcolm Miller*, a 300-ton schooner, and part of the experience is that you are one of the **(13)** ..... – a pleasure for which you pay quite a lot. Hebridean Island Cruises offer a variety of cruises to many of the most beautiful spots on the western seaboard in the *Hebridean Princess*, a luxury floating hotel with a crew of thirty **(14)** ..... forty passengers. If you're lucky with the weather and can **(15)** ..... it, this could be the ideal holiday for you.

0	**A**	action	**(B)**	activity	**C**	act	**D**	acting
1	**A**	prospectus	**B**	catalogue	**C**	brochure	**D**	journal
2	**A**	data	**B**	facts	**C**	information	**D**	details
3	**A**	visit	**B**	contact	**C**	write	**D**	know
4	**A**	invited	**B**	referred	**C**	introduced	**D**	presented
5	**A**	situations	**B**	sites	**C**	sights	**D**	sightings
6	**A**	practices	**B**	studies	**C**	careers	**D**	courses
7	**A**	relaxation	**B**	learning	**C**	improvement	**D**	recuperation
8	**A**	amount	**B**	quality	**C**	capacity	**D**	quantity
9	**A**	sailing	**B**	water-skiing	**C**	stone-cutting	**D**	chess
10	**A**	experts	**B**	sports	**C**	activities	**D**	enthusiasts
11	**A**	bank	**B**	shore	**C**	coast	**D**	seaside
12	**A**	set	**B**	run	**C**	take	**D**	stage
13	**A**	group	**B**	staff	**C**	team	**D**	crew
14	**A**	to look after	**B**	to help	**C**	to treat	**D**	to take on
15	**A**	buy	**B**	afford	**C**	pay	**D**	spend

Part 2

For questions **16–30**, complete the following article by writing each missing word on the answer sheet. **Use only one word for each space**. The exercise begins with an example **(0)**.

Example:

0	as	0 __

CARROT ADDICTION

Eating carrots may be as addictive as cigarette smoking and every bit **(0)** ..... difficult to give up, according to recent research. **(16)** ..... it has been known since **(17)** ..... early 1900s that excessive carrot intake can turn the skin orange, the psychological effects of **(18)** ..... behaviour are only **(19)** ..... coming to light. One woman patient **(20)** ..... was eating a kilogram of raw carrots a day had to be treated in a psychiatric hospital. Another woman started consuming huge quantities of carrots **(21)** ..... pregnant and managed to stop for 15 years after the baby was born. The habit resumed **(22)** ..... an illness when she resorted **(23)** ..... buying and eating carrots secretly. Switching to **(24)** ..... vegetable helped reduce her dependency. She now survives happily **(25)** ..... a carrot-free diet. Another case concerns a man who sought help to give up tobacco. His wife advised him to replace smoking **(26)** ..... eating vegetables. He was soon consuming up **(27)** ..... five bunches of carrots a day. The man abandoned the carrot habit. **(28)** ..... , he resumed smoking. One researcher suggests that the psychological dependence arises not only from the carotene contained in the vegetable, but also from some other ingredient. He says that the withdrawal symptoms are **(29)** ..... intense that the addicts get hold of and consume carrots **(30)** ..... in socially unacceptable situations!

Part 3

In **most** lines of the following text, there is **one** unnecessary word. It is either grammatically incorrect or does not fit in with the sense of the text. For each numbered line **31–46**, find this word and then write it in the box on your answer sheet. **Some lines are correct**. Indicate these with a tick (✓) in the box. The exercise begins with two examples **(0)**, and **(00)**.

Examples:

0	and	0
00	✓	0

COMMUNICATION

0	Managers spend most of their time communicating – reading, and writing,
00	talking or listening – yet the evidence is that they do not always do this
31	as successfully. One reason that has been suggested for this is that, in the
32	past, communication was regarded as a natural process, not been taught
33	in any formal sense. This theory has been changing, and with the concept
34	of communication as an 'art' now appears regularly in the management
35	courses and seminars. Communication is probably only one of the least
36	appreciated aspects of management, and more and more organisations are
37	realising that effective communication involves telling staff why all things
38	are happening. This not only helps day-to-day working but allows changes
39	to be introduced more smoothly, and sometimes leads to improvements for
40	being mentioned by staff. Both the morale and efficiency of an organisation
41	are depend to a great extent on the abilities of its staff to communicate
42	effectively. Communication is not something that should be undertaken
43	only when trouble occurs. It should be a daily habit if the organisation is
44	to run smoothly and avoid difficulties and, of course, it should be both a
45	two-way process, involving listening to as well as talking. Regular exchanges
46	of ideas between managers and staff will be help to create good teamwork.

Part 4

For questions **47–61**, read the two texts on pages **98–99**. Use the words in the boxes to the right of the text, listed **47–61**, to form a word that fits in the same numbered space in the text. Write the new word in the correct box on your answer sheet. The exercise begins with an example **(0)**.

Example:

0	increasingly	0

BOOK REVIEW

BUYING A COMPUTER GUIDE

Thinking of buying a computer?

Computers are playing an **(0)** ..... important part in our lives, both in our homes and at work. But how do you know which computer will suit your needs? This practical, straight-forward and **(47)** ..... guide, especially designed for those who are not **(48)** ..... about computers, provides many clear **(49)** ..... of all the jargon. It makes a **(50)** ..... of various systems, tells you how much you should pay, how to avoid costly mistakes and how to get **(51)** ..... user support and maintenance. This fact-packed book is essential reading for anyone planning to buy a computer. Giving advice which is not **(52)** ..... , it will ensure that you make the right choice. Altogether, an invaluable **(53)** ..... .

(0)	INCREASE
(47)	RELY
(48)	KNOWLEDGE
(49)	EXPLAIN
(50)	COMPARE
(51)	SATISFY
(52)	BIAS
(53)	PUBLISH

MAGAZINE ARTICLE

IT IS NEVER TOO LATE TO BE PUNCTUAL

People who are unpunctual fall into three categories. The first, and **(54)** ..... , comprises the **(55)** ..... incompetent and **(56)** ..... who worry about being on time and never are. The second lot are, strange as it may seem, **(57)** ..... people who cannot bear to be kept waiting, and who make sure they aren't by always being late themselves, thus **(58)** ..... that others must wait for them. If they are outmanoeuvred and compelled to wait for someone, they are the first to express **(59)** ..... of the bad manners of the latecomers. Finally, there are the egoists, determined to impose their own personality on others and to impress their sense of **(60)** ..... on them. An easy way to do this is to keep everyone waiting until the star makes an **(61)** ..... .

(54)	SAD
(55)	HOPELESS
(56)	EFFICIENT
(57)	PATIENCE
(58)	GUARANTEE
(59)	APPROVE
(60)	IMPORTANT
(61)	APPEAR

Part 5

For questions **62–74**, read the formal regulations about fire safety and use the information in this text to complete the numbered gaps in the informal instructions to employees. Then write the new words in the correct spaces on your answer sheet. **Use no more than two words** for each gap. The words you need **do not** occur in the formal regulations. The exercise begins with an example **(0)**.

Example:

0	you see	0

EXTRACT FROM COMPANY REGULATIONS

PROCEDURES IN CASE OF FIRE

Should a fire commence and be observed then a decision must be taken as to whether it is feasible to make an attempt to extinguish it. If the person who discovers the fire makes the judgement that it cannot be dealt with alone, and in a reasonable period of time, then the firebell should be rung to alert others. It is recommended that every employee, on hearing the firebell ring, should immediately cease whatever activity he or she is engaged in, and vacate the room in order to effect an escape via the route which is indicated on the plan displayed in every office. In the event of any employee discovering the stairway blocked or filled with smoke, he or she should use the external fire escape forthwith and in no circumstances consider making use of the lifts. It is imperative that no employee returns to the building, however urgent or necessary this may appear to be, unless authorised to do so by the fire officer. Employees should await instructions as to when they may re-enter the building.

INSTRUCTIONS TO EMPLOYEES

FIRE – WHAT YOU SHOULD DO!

If **(0)** ..... a fire start, decide whether it is safe for you to try to put **(62)** ..... .
Don't deal with the fire on **(63)** ..... if it seems too much for you, or you
think you cannot cope with it fairly **(64)** ..... . Let everyone know there is a
fire by ringing the firebell! As **(65)** ..... you hear the firebell, you should
immediately **(66)** ..... what you are doing and **(67)** ..... of the building.
(68) ..... the safest route by looking at the plan on the wall in your office. If you
(69) ..... the stairs blocked or filled with smoke, immediately use the fire
escape which can be found on the **(70)** ..... the building. Using the lifts
can be extremely dangerous, so don't even for one moment **(71)** ..... using
them. Once you are out of the building, don't **(72)** ..... in for anything,
unless the fire officer tells you it is **(73)** ..... to do so. You should then wait
until you **(74)** ..... by the fire officer that you can go back to work.

Part 6

For questions **75–80**, read the following text and then choose from the list **A–J** the best phrase given below to fill each of the spaces. Write one letter **(A–J)** in the correct box on your answer sheet. Each correct phrase may only be used once. **Some of the suggested answers do not fit at all.** The exercise begins with an example **(0)**.

Example:

THE CHINESE IN THE USA

In 1848, gold was discovered in California. Within a year, the territory had attracted vast numbers of people from other countries. They came from every part of the globe – Australia, France, Turkey and China. Their plan was to work until they had enough money **(0)** ..... .

   As the gold began to run out, the Chinese were still able **(75)** ..... . They would run laundries, grow vegetables and do construction work. In the 1860s, there was a railway boom. The government provided money to build railways **(76)** ..... . Again, labour was needed and the Chinese arrived in large numbers. By 1870, some 100,000 Chinese had arrived in California and the vast majority decided **(77)** ..... . In San Francisco, the Chinese lived together in a section of that city which became known as Chinatown. There, they were able **(78)** ..... , such as the Chinese New Year celebrations.

   Today, individual Chinese-Americans have achieved success in ways quite different from the work done by the first immigrants. The computer scientist, Dr An Wang, for example, is now the fifth wealthiest man in the United States. The wealth generated by his business has enabled him **(79)** ..... , including student exchanges between the United States and China. He has also established the Wang Institute of Graduate Studies, one of only three schools in the country **(80)** ..... . His family has come a long way in a hundred years.

A to struggle to achieve recognition

B to find opportunities to work

C to finance many philanthropic projects

D to spend the rest of their lives there

E to maintain their traditions and customs

F to be found in other cities also

G to celebrate their achievements

H to offer a Masters degree in software engineering

I to link the east and west coasts

J to return home wealthy

PAPER 4   LISTENING (45 minutes approximately)

Part 1

You will hear part of a radio programme in which details of a competition are announced. For questions **1–9**, complete the notes.

You will hear the recording **twice**.

YOUNG ENTREPRENEUR

Competition open to people aged 18 to 25.

Organised through a programme called **[1]**

Last year's competition won by a Turk who runs a **[2]**

He was chosen from **[3]** finalists.

All finalists are **[4]**

Entry: – must be typed on one side of paper only

   – no longer than **[5]**

   – must have a person's signature

   – person must not be **[6]**

Include name, home and business addresses and **[7]**

Closing date: **[8]**

Final prizewinner's name broadcast in **[9]** programme.

Part 2

You will hear a local radio broadcast about transport and travel. For questions **10–16**, complete the notes using no more than three words in each gap.

Listen very carefully as you will hear the recording ONCE only.

- Roadworks causing delays on approach to [**10**]

- Stadley: station closed due to [**11**]

  buses available for those with [**12**]

- Main road through Chorley village is [**13**]

- Airport is open, no [**14**] but several

  international flights [**15**]

- City centre bomb scare still causing [**16**]

Part 3

Your will hear part of a radio programme about dancing. For questions **17–22**, choose the correct answer **A, B, C** or **D.**

You will hear the recording **twice**.

17
What makes Shirley dance?
A   certain types of music
B   other people dancing
C   the beat of music
D   being in a good mood

18
How does Tony choose which song to play first?
A   according to the age of the crowd
B   according to the atmosphere in the place
C   according to musical fashions at the time
D   according to the type of event it is

19
What happens at some company dances, according to Tony?
A   People feel obliged to dance.
B   The bosses don't dance.
C   There is more talking than dancing.
D   People are too shy to dance.

20
According to Emma, why is dancing important to young people?
A   It gives them a sense of identity.
B   It reflects their cultural background.
C   They have more energy than older people.
D   They gain a greater understanding of music.

21
Emma believes that musical taste
A   shows there are no barriers between people.
B   is a reflection of cultural influences.
C   reflects people's political views.
D   shows how individual people are.

22
What is Tony's opinion of dancing?
A   It brings all social classes together.
B   It makes young people happy.
C   It enables people to make friends.
D   It can be enjoyed by everyone.

Part 4

You will hear five short extracts in which different people are talking about performances that they have been to. For questions **23–32**, choose the correct answer **A, B** or **C**.

You will hear the recording **twice**.

23
The concert was unusual because the musicians didn't use
A   microphones.
B   instruments.
C   a stage.

24
In talking about the concert, the speaker says she
A   hadn't heard that kind of music before.
B   hadn't really liked the music.
C   hadn't understood the music very well.

25
What does the speaker say about the concert?
A   The musicians were very old.
B   The songs were too unfamiliar.
C   The sound quality was poor.

26
The audience were
A   appreciative.
B   dissatisfied.
C   inattentive.

27
What does the speaker say about the theatre?
A   It had recently moved.
B   It was overcrowded.
C   It was unusually small.

28
The play was spoilt because the actors
A   forgot their lines.
B   were unenthusiastic.
C   had too much make-up on.

29
At the start of the concert, the speaker was surprised by the number of
A   people who arrived late.
B   people he recognised.
C   female performers.

30
What section of the orchestra did the speaker find disappointing?
A   the violins
B   the brass
C   the drums

31
The acrobatic acts were
A   impressive.
B   alarming.
C   repetitive.

32
How did the speaker feel at the end of the performance?
A   She didn't realise it was so late.
B   She felt it should have ended earlier.
C   She would have preferred an evening ticket.

(This test is also suitable for groups of three students; this only occurs as the last test of a session where a centre has an uneven number of candidates. It takes about 23 minutes.)

PAPER 5   SPEAKING (15 minutes)

There are two examiners. One (the Interlocutor) conducts the test, providing you with the necessary materials and explaining what you have to do. The other examiner (the Assessor) will be introduced to you, but then takes no further part in the interaction.

Part 1 (3 minutes for pairs of candidates, 5 minutes for groups of three)
The Interlocutor will first ask you and your partner(s) a few questions. You will then be asked to find out some information about each other, on topics such as hobbies, interests, career plans, etc.

Part 2 (4 minutes for pairs of candidates, 6 minutes for groups of three)
You will each be given the opportunity to talk for about a minute, and to comment briefly after your partners have spoken.

The Interlocutor gives you a set of photographs and asks you to talk about them for about one minute.

You will then be given another set of photographs to look at. One of your partners talks about these photographs for about one minute.

If a group of three students is being tested, the Interlocutor will give you all another two photographs to look at. The final student talks about these photographs for a minute.

When you have all had your turn, the Interlocutor will ask you to look at each other's pictures again and answer another question, which relates to the photographs.

Part 3 (4 minutes for pairs of candidates, 6 minutes for groups of three)
In this part of the test you and your partner(s) will be asked to talk together. The Interlocutor will place a new set of pictures on the table in front of you. This stimulus provides the basis for a discussion. The Interlocutor will explain what you have to do.

Part 4 (4 minutes for pairs of candidates, 6 minutes for groups of three)
The Interlocutor will ask some further questions, which will lead to a more general discussion of what you have talked about in Part 3 and in which you will be encouraged to comment on what your partner(s) say(s).

Test 1 Key

Paper 1   Reading (1 hour 15 minutes)

Part 1

1 A   2 A/E   3 A/E   4 B/D   5 B/D   6 C   7 G   8 A
9 F/H   10 F/H   11 E   12 B   13 E   14 H   15 G

Part 2

16 H   17 B   18 G   19 A   20 D   21 F   22 C

Part 3

23 B   24 C   25 C   26 B   27 D

Part 4

28 A   29 E   30 B   31 C   32 A/E   33 A/E
34 B/E   35 B/E   36 B   37 C   38 A   39 E
40 A/B/D   41 A/B/D   42 A/B/D   43 B   44 E   45 D

Paper 2 Writing (2 hours)

Task-specific mark schemes

Question 1

Content (points covered)
Two letters
(a)   A letter with at least a balanced reference to three points:
  • description of what happened
  • conveyance of thanks
  • offer of repayment of costs.
  Letters that do not mention ALL three can only get a mark of 2.
  Suitable opening/close to letter, with appropriate introductory statement
  of who the writer is.
(b)   A brief letter summarising the outcome, not merely a list of contents.
  Should mention reference number, and must refer to missing passport to
  get a minimum mark of 3.
NB   Candidates must do both (a) and (b) for a minimum mark of 3.

Organisation and cohesion
(a)   Correct letter format (addresses not necessary) with clear paragraphs.
  Cohesive devices used effectively to link the details of the incident, the
  expression of thanks and the offer to repay the cost.

(b) One paragraph sufficient, but well-balanced. Succinct emphasis on the passport being missing. Appropriate opening and closing statements.

Range

Shows clear contrast in expression between (a) and (b), avoiding repetition. Minimal lifting from the question paper with some paraphrasing.

   Evidence of use of original expressions appropriate to each letter with competent use of both factual language and personal expression. Ability to summarise describing events clearly.

Register

(a) Formal – could be fairly informal, but polite/consistent.
(b) Formal/neutral.

Target reader

(a) Editor would be informed and interested enough to publish the letter.
(b) The police would be informed of the loss of the passport and connect it to the original incident.

Question 2

Content (points covered)

Clear summary including name of the book in question. For a minimum mark of 3, all three basic aspects of the task have to be included – name of book and summary, why others might enjoy it and what can be learned from it.
NB Book can be of any type (not only literature) but must be in English.

Organisation and cohesion

A purposeful opening and brief conclusion – an attempt to engage readers from the beginning. Cohesive connections of summary and other two points. Review format, not letter.

   Paragraphs and/or sub-headings for three basic aspects, although second and third aspects may well be linked, and even embedded in the summary.

   Ability to summarise, describing clearly what the book is about.

Range

Competent use of both factual language and the language of personal opinion. (The language of literary criticism is not expected.)

Register

Neutral or informal, appropriate to the chosen target audience – consistent. Some enthusiasm should be evident with a possible touch of rhetoric.

Target reader

Reader would be sufficiently informed and interested to form an opinion on the book and decide whether to read it.

Question 3

Content (points covered)
Should be 'anchored' geographically, mentioning country, and should be a contemporary challenge.
Should be a challenge faced by *young* people, not just the general public.
Candidates who write about more than one challenge may not fully complete task envisaged. If candidates interpret 'challenge' as 'problem', they should not automatically be penalised.

Organisation and cohesion
Appropriate paragraphing with a clear introduction and conclusion and a title other than Project 2000. There should be an attempt to engage readers from the beginning.

Range
Interesting opening with some original language. Relevant vocabulary (to whatever challenge is) and correct use of future tenses.
  Narrative/descriptive language and some expressions of rhetoric or personal opinion.

Register
Fairly formal/neutral. Could be neutral/informal if young people's magazine.

Target reader
Readers of international magazine would be informed and interested.

Question 4

Content (points covered)
Proposal must cover the three bullet points:
- what places the video should show and why
- who it would be interesting to have interviewed on the video and why
- what is special about the character of candidate's town/city that the video should try to convey
NB i)   Reason(s) for including particular places or interviews could be embedded in the naming/description(s) of choice(s).
    ii) Any reasonable interpretation of 'special' – subjective or objective – is acceptable; it is not necessary to show the town/city has proven cultural/national significance.

Organisation and cohesion
The proposal should be clearly organised with suitable paragraphing. Acceptable to use letter or report format, with or without headings and sub-headings.

Range
Description, opinion, and language of explanation.
  Vocabulary relating to town/city life, atmosphere, human character and/or achievement.

Register
Consistently formal or neutral.

Target reader
Would be clearly informed about possible approaches to making a video of the candidate's town/city – and able to assess the recommendations seriously for substance and interest.

Question 5

Content (points covered)
Clear introduction explaining purpose of report.
Description of one specific location in another country, which should be stated. (Inappropriate to dwell exclusively on anecdotal experiences in a place, especially negative ones. Factual approach needed, not personal experience.)
For a mark of 3, the two basic aspects of the task have to be included:
• location, giving geographical details
• why it is suitable.
Any relevant feature (including communications, etc.) is acceptable.

Organisation and cohesion
Report format, not letter.
Clear layout, with possible sub-headings, and obvious paragraphing. Clear introduction explaining purpose of report. An introductory sentence in 'letter format' is acceptable.

Range
Vocabulary and structures appropriate for suggestion/recommendations and a clear explanation of why a location is suitable. Language describing a business situation. (Not necessarily complex structures.) 'Business' terminology appropriate to a proposal.

Register
Formal/neutral.

Target reader
Would understand all the points being made and have enough information to evaluate the choice of location.

Paper 3 English in Use (1 hour 30 minutes)

Part 1
1 D   2 A   3 B   4 C   5 D   6 A   7 A   8 A   9 C
10 A   11 B   12 A   13 D   14 B   15 A

Part 2
16 be   17 though/however   18 to   19 others/some/many/several
20 that/which   21 with   22 such   23 or   24 but   25 so
26 for   27 on/upon   28 which   29 long   30 suddenly/quickly

Part 3

31 ✓   32 of   33 it   34 ✓   35 to   36 round   37 ✓
38 about   39 soon   40 for   41 not   42 ✓   43 could
44 them   45 ✓   46 out

Part 4

47 increasingly   48 repetition   49 variety   50 significant
51 memorizing/memorising   52 personally   53 underestimate
54 scientists   55 global   56 ecological   57 admission
58 additional   59 subscription   60 membership   61 reduction(s)

Part 5

62 taking over   63 offered   64 a degree/a qualification/qualifications
65 head/leader   66 area/field   67 so well
68 under you/to manage   69 trips abroad   70 (very) good/excellent
71 cost much   72 discuss it   73 depends on
74 arrive/be received/be in

Part 6

75 H   76 C   77 G   78 I   79 B   80 D

Paper 4 Listening (approximately 45 minutes)

Part 1

1 a chemist's (shop)/chemist shop   2 1837
3 genuine and original
4 unwell/ill/sick/not (very) well
5 (the) West Indies   6 only four/4 people/employees
7 30,000 litres   8 three/3 years   9 long neck   10 glass

Part 2

11 1400 hrs/2 pm   12 (approximately/just under) $3\frac{1}{2}$ hour(s)/3 hrs 30 min
13 (very) comfortable/fine/OK   14 meal(s) (*plus*) wine
15 (£) 20 (per) booking   16 refunded/returned/repaid (at ferry office)
17 every/each hour
18 (ferry) ticket(s) (as a proof)

Part 3

19 C   20 C   21 B   22 D   23 B   24 D   25 C   26 A

Part 4

27 A   28 E   29 H   30 G   31 D
32 H   33 F   34 C   35 G   36 E

Transcript   *This is the Cambridge Certificate in Advanced English Listening Test. Test One.*

This paper requires you to listen to a selection of recorded material and answer the accompanying questions.

*There are four parts to the test, **One, Two, Three** and **Four**. You will hear Part Two **once** only. All the other parts of the test will be heard twice.*

There will be a pause before each part to allow you to look through the questions, and other pauses to let you think about your answers. At the end of every pause you will hear this sound.

tone

*You should write your answers on the **question** paper. You will have **ten** minutes at the end to **transfer your answers to the separate answer sheet**.*

The tape will now be stopped. You must ask any questions now as you will not be allowed to speak during the test.

[pause]

PART 1   *Now open your question paper and look at Part One.*

[pause]

Part One
You will hear a talk about a product called Akwaaba Sauce. For questions 1 to 10, complete the notes. You will hear the recording twice.

[pause]

tone

Announcer: ... And now Joan Yates discovers the origins of Akwaaba sauce.
Presenter: The Australians say it's absolutely brilliant on barbecues, the French claim it brings out the piquancy of steak tartare and there's nothing the Chinese like better than to dip their dim sum in it. In fact, Akwaaba sauce is a product that's on the tip of just about everyone's tongue.

  Maurice Bond started it all on his return to the town of Charlton in England from India in 1835. At a chemist's shop in Tower Street he handed over a secret recipe for a special spicy sauce. Mr John Ford was behind the counter and so was Mr William Stott. They had the knowledge, they concocted the ingredients and they kept a little for themselves. One day, when they were clearing the cellar out, they found it, dusted it off, brought it back up, tried it and eureka – Akwaaba sauce.

  They then began commercial production in 1837, each bottle bearing the words 'genuine and original' on labels. A High Court order would later prevent other sauce manufacturers from using these words. In 1904 came royal approval – the ultimate acclaim – and with the help of explorers, Akwaaba sauce started to reach many parts of the world. For example, a Colonel Middleton was on his way to China and he stopped off in Tibet to pay his respects to the high priest, the High Lama.

  He found that the poor old High Lama was not very well, so he left him some of the sauce and proceeded on his way. He came back some two or three years later,

113

called in to see how things were and, lo and behold, the High Lama had made a miraculous recovery.

Until the 1950s Akwaaba sauce bottles were hand-wrapped in special paper. In the US, they continue the tradition to this day. The ingredients are on the bottle for all to see – molasses from the West Indies, anchovies from the Mediterranean, tamarinds from India. But what happens to these ingredients behind the closed doors of the Akwaaba factory remains a closely guarded secret known only to four key employees. Inside the 'making house', in vats holding 30,000 litres, the young sauce is matured for months on end. In two other locations there are the lines of 'maturation vessels', in which the separate ingredients stand for three years. Eventually, they're brought together and slowly stirred.

They produce twelve million bottles a year in the UK alone and they make it under licence in the US, Canada and Australia. Its shelf life, they claim, is indefinite. They still pass on the original recipe by word of mouth and they still retain the distinctive long-necked glass chemist's bottle. After all, to change the design or go for plastic would be to change a winning formula.

[pause]

tone

Now you will hear the recording again.

[The recording is repeated.]

[pause]

That is the end of Part One.

[pause]

PART 2

Part Two
You will hear an announcement about a change in transport arrangements. For questions 11 to 18, complete the notes the speaker is using. Listen very carefully as you will hear the recording ONCE only.

[pause]

tone

Announcer: Good morning ladies and gentlemen. First of all, on behalf of Seeways Midland let me apologise for keeping you waiting so long. I realise that you have been severely inconvenienced. The ferry will be sailing at 1400 hours, that's two o'clock this afternoon. Journey time is estimated at just under three and a half hours. You will be entitled to compensation and hopefully you will be at your destination soon. We have organised a relief ferry, the Sealife. Passengers who booked cabins will unfortunately not be able to have cabins on the relief ferry as this is an older vessel and does not have cabin facilities. It is, however, a very comfortable ship so please don't worry. On board you will all be entitled to a free meal with free wine, for those that want it.

On the subject of compensation: passengers will receive a fixed sum of twenty pounds per booking from Seeways, that's twenty pounds per booking, not per person. Oh yes, and those passengers that booked cabins will have the cabin surcharge refunded to them at the ferry offices at the same time, on production of the cabin ticket. Plus you can claim ten pounds for every hour that you had to wait, which will be paid by the travel insurance company – Medway Insurance, not Seeways, but Medway and their address is on your tickets. Please do not apply to the ferry company for this allowance. You can collect your £20 voucher from the Seeways office on arrival at your port of entry to Britain. Please have your tickets with you as proof of your booking; passengers without tickets will not be entitled to this compensation.

Please accept my apologies again – hopefully the dispute which has caused the delay will be settled soon. I do wish you a pleasant voyage and thank you for your co-operation.

[pause]

That is the end of Part Two.

[pause]

PART 3

Part Three
You will hear a woman on a radio programme interviewing a driving instructor about his job. For questions 19 to 26, choose the correct answer A, B, C or D. You will hear the recording twice.

[pause]

tone

Interviewer:	We've invited Fred Watson, a driving instructor with over 20 years' experience to talk to us about learning to drive. Well, Fred, I suppose you must find your job frustrating at times!
Fred Watson:	Not at all. I enjoy it most of the time, but of course, you do get the odd difficult customer. Most people are very impatient to pass the test as quickly as possible in order to keep their expenditure down.
Interviewer:	Would you say it's expensive to learn to drive these days then?
Fred Watson:	Well, it depends on several things. If you come to a private instructor like me, it's probably going to be a bit less expensive than going to one of the big schools. The thing is, people have usually heard of the big schools and trust their reputation, whereas I tend to rely more on personal recommendations.
Interviewer:	Does that mean you have to try harder to get customers?
Fred Watson:	Not now. When I started I had to, but in fact I'm fully booked at the moment as my prices are quite competitive.
Interviewer:	Learning to drive is usually regarded as a rather nerve-racking experience for the learner. What do you think?
Fred Watson:	Well, it can be! But I try to get my clients to unwind before the lesson. I ask them to sit quietly in the driver's seat for a few moments with their eyes closed. You'd be surprised how it changes some people. They feel much more ready to drive if they've had a few quiet moments.
Interviewer:	Yes. I suppose some people are more nervous than others. What would you say makes people most nervous?
Fred Watson:	Hard to say. Probably it's the fear of not being able to react fast enough. At first they're trying to master the controls of the car. Then they start worrying about whether they're in the right part of the road and whether they have signalled in time and so on.

Interviewer:	Yes, there seem to be so many things to remember at once. I remember thinking I'd never master all of it however long I practised.
Fred Watson:	Usually people master the controls fairly quickly, but they have to think more about what they're doing and until it feels almost automatic, they still make silly mistakes which occasionally lead to accidents.
Interviewer:	So how soon can you let a pupil take total control of the car?
Fred Watson:	It differs from one person to another, of course, but generally speaking I allow them to drive without dual control when I'm certain they can use the gears correctly, stop in an emergency and have reasonable awareness of other road-users.
Interviewer:	What kind of person makes a good driver then?
Fred Watson:	You're asking me to commit myself here, aren't you? Well, first of all, let me say I have no evidence to suggest that either men or women are better drivers. What I would say, though, is that a certain level of confidence is necessary, a belief that you can and will succeed, but it's dangerous to be over-confident and you can end up making wrong decisions. I'm afraid some young people are over-enthusiastic and start by driving too fast and taking risks. Now I have to warn them that this approach is not going to make them into a good driver. What I like to see is someone who is prepared to take time and patience to develop the skill.
Interviewer:	Do you think intelligence has anything to do with it?
Fred Watson:	Depends how you define it – do you mean academic ability or practical good sense?
Interviewer:	Well, I suppose I'm asking you whether either of these is relevant.
Fred Watson:	Practical good sense, alertness and confidence are more important, but you also need a reasonable memory as you have to get through the part of the test where you recognise signs and symbols. And of course you need to know them when you're a driver out there on your own.
Interviewer:	Yes. And with the volume of cars on the road today, quick reactions are essential too.
Fred Watson:	That's right. Driving is getting more demanding all the time, so we must make sure people learn efficiently in the first place, and give them value for money.
Interviewer:	Well, I'm sure Fred's pupils are getting value for money. Thank you for talking to us, Fred – and good luck to all you listeners who are about to take your driving test.

[pause]

tone

Now you will hear the recording again.

[The recording is repeated.]

[pause]

That is the end of Part Three.

[pause]

PART 4

Part Four
This part consists of two tasks. You will hear various people talking about the experience of winning something. Look at Task One.
For questions 27 to 31, match the extracts as you hear them with the people listed A to H.

Now look at Task Two. For questions 32 to 36, match the extracts as you hear them with the topics listed A to H.

You will hear the recording twice. While you listen you must complete both tasks.

[pause]

tone

Man: It was such a wonderful surprise when the letter arrived. I'd sent in a couple of pictures I'd taken in the garden while I was still in work and then forgotten about it. You never think it could really happen to you, do you? The money certainly came in handy until I found something else.

Woman: I was very sceptical when she first started going in for them. You know, when they're at that age and get these ideas you worry, don't you? I'd never really seen her as exceptionally clever or well-read. I suppose you don't with your own. She certainly doesn't get her brains from me and that's for sure!

Man: Well, we only started to play when we stopped working and we certainly never intended to go in for competitions. It's a game that suits people of our age, sort of slow moving, but good exercise. And then we both found that we not only enjoyed it but were rather good at it and so now we've got this cup. It's strange really.

Man: I don't know why mine turn out better than anyone else's. Perhaps it's something to do with the soil and of course it's not only a matter of size. To win they have to be perfect in every way and that comes from a lot of loving care and attention.

Woman: The idea came to me one day in the garden as I was jotting down a few ideas. I thought what would I do if I won a lot of money? Would it ruin everything or would it be a new beginning? It's ironic that it should win, but literary prizes are not in the big league financially, so I won't be having any of those problems myself.

[pause]

tone

Now you will hear the recording again. Remember, you must complete both tasks.

[The recording is repeated.]

[pause]

*That is the end of Part Four. There will now be a ten minute pause to allow you to **transfer your answers to the separate answer sheet**. Be sure to follow the numbering of all the questions. The question papers and answer sheets will then be collected by your supervisor.*

Teacher, pause the tape here for ten minutes. Remind your students when they have one minute left.

That is the end of the test.

Test 2 Key

Paper 1 Reading (1 hour 15 minutes)

Part 1

1 A   2 D/E   3 D/E   4 D   5 A/B   6 A/B   7 C   8 B/G
9 B/G   10 E/F   11 E/F   12 C   13 E   14 C

Part 2

15 D   16 F   17 E   18 G   19 B   20 C

Part 3

21 C   22 B   23 B   24 A   25 C

Part 4

26 C   27 B/E   28 B/E   29 B   30 D   31 C/D   32 C/D
33 A   34 B/D   35 B/D   36 A/E   37 A/E   38 C   39 E
40 C   41 B   42 A

Paper 2 Writing (2 hours)

Task-specific mark schemes

Question 1

Content (points covered)
Two letters
(a) Explanation of who is writing and why. Reference to the advertisement. The application must deal with the four points in the advertisement: type of placement; when person is available; academic and/or work experience; benefits to be gained. Should also cover the skills in Sheila's letter, i.e. level of English, computer skills and connections with Zimbabwe (Sheila). Should **not** ask about expenses or a place to stay, as these are to be covered in Letter B.
(b) Description of the action taken, but should avoid repetition of Letter A. Request for advice about where to stay and what would be a reasonable amount of expenses. Friendly greetings.
   Both letters must be attempted for a minimum mark of 3.

Organisation and cohesion
(a) Clear introduction. Paragraphs should group the information and ideas appropriately. Standard closing formula for an application.
(b) Brief – perhaps two paragraphs.

118

Range
(a) Language to give information. Persuasion. Some use of future tenses.
Vocabulary to do with aspect of working life and work abroad.
(b) Friendly expressions and requesting advice.

Register
(a) Formal.
(b) Informal.

Target reader
(a) Would have a clear picture of the applicant and know whether he/she was suitable.
(b) Would be pleased to receive the letter and be fully informed.

Question 2

Content (points covered)
Description of **more than one** family celebration remembered from childhood.
Explanation of how such celebrations might be different for children today.
NB Both the description (more than one celebration) and the explanation
must be covered for a minimum mark of 3.

Organisation and cohesion
Title an advantage. Strong opening and ending. Different organisation possible:
a paragraph on each celebration, including comparison with today OR
paragraph(s) on the celebrations, followed by a paragraph on today.

Range
Language of description and past tense narrative (habitual past, e.g. 'used to' or
'would'). Language of comparison and contrast. Vocabulary relating to
celebrations, if necessary with some explanation of local terms.

Register
Consistently semi-formal or formal.

Target reader
Would be interested and informed.

Question 3

Content (points covered)
Contribution should cover what to do and see in the countryside; where to
stay; what the weather might be like. Area should be part of candidate's own
country. As this is a contribution, area need not necessarily be named. Should
be positive about the undiscovered nature of these places.
NB All three elements must be covered for a minimum mark of 3.

Organisation and cohesion
Continuous test with some sub-headings and/or clear paragraphing.

Range
Language of description and recommendation. Positive expressions. Vocabulary relating to travel and tourism.

Register
Neutral or semi-formal. **NB** Not appropriate to write in first person.

Target reader
Would be fully informed about the area.

Question 4

Content (points covered)
Report should cover the two questions (both for a minimum mark of 3): *Are today's young people watching too much TV?; What influences (good or bad) does TV have on the young?* Must relate to candidate's own area. Mention of the survey and who the fifty people were, including their ages. Some inclusion of number references or percentages.

Organisation and cohesion
Report format, though acceptable to begin as a letter. Clear paragraphing and/or sub-headings. Concluding paragraph.

Range
Language of description and giving information. Some evaluation/conclusions drawn from the survey findings. Use of number language. Vocabulary relating to entertainment and free time.

Register
Formal.

Target reader
Would have sufficient information about the candidate's area.

Question 5

Content (points covered)
Memo should cover own opinions and those of colleagues, thus including both positive and negative points. Mention of the course and the accommodation and other facilities (candidate to specify these). Recommendation or otherwise to senior colleague about the course. Commiserations about colleague's illness.

Organisation and cohesion
Sub-headings would be useful – memo should clearly differentiate the content elements and there should be a concluding paragraph at the end.

Range
Language of description. Some language of personal opinion and the reporting of other people's opinions. Evaluate expressions. Polite commiserating. Vocabulary to do with work and training.

Register
Formal.

Target reader
Would be cheered to see that she hadn't missed much and would have an accurate picture of the course.

Paper 3 English in Use (1 hour 30 minutes)

Part 1

1 C   2 D   3 A   4 B   5 B   6 D   7 B   8 A   9 C
10 D   11 C   12 D   13 A   14 C   15 B

Part 2

16 in   17 there   18 how   19 with   20 had   21 that/which
22 All   23 were   24 being   25 much/considerably/far   26 than
27 same   28 does/will   29 well   30 if/when

Part 3

31 Moore, explained   32 migratory   33 ✓   34 dropped
35 ✓   36 sites   37 ✓   38 until   39 achieved? The   40 of
41 sources   42 ✓   43 achieved, work   44 "We   45 account
46 we'll

Part 4

47 unimportant   48 fully   49 requirements   50 alphabetically
51 entry   52 surprisingly   53 subjective   54 currently
55 measurements   56 specialists   57 receipt   58 precise
59 populated   60 collection   61 hourly

Part 5

62 a maximum   63 in mind   64 humour/wit   65 high cost
66 is enclosed   67 no limit   68 be awarded/given/presented
69 accompanied   70 fee   71 reduced   72 local
73 closing date/deadline   74 announced/made public

Part 6

75 I   76 C   77 G   78 E   79 B   80 A

Paper 4 Listening (45 minutes approximately)

Part 1

1 exhibition of portraits/photographs   2 Theatre Royal
3 As You Like It   4 (season of) classic films/movies   5 As They Were
6 Media Centre, Bristol   7 The Disappearing Act   8 Out of the Wood
9 Literature Festival   10 Ways With Words

Part 2

11 (the) Red Room   12 (the) Bicycle Museum   13 (indoor) market
14 (an) open-air/outdoor restaurant   15 (as) river trip
16 (the) Wooden House

Part 3

17 unpleasant/uncomfortable/formal/of an ordeal
18 his (own) children/family   19 easy/simple   20 the background(s)
21 play up to it/the camera *or* react/pose
22 anger/bad temper   23 video technology
24 collecting pictures/photos *or* making collections/putting collections together

Part 4

25 B   26 C   27 H   28 D   29 F
30 F   31 H   32 C   33 E   34 A

Transcript   *This is the Cambridge Certificate in Advanced English Listening Test. Test Two.*

This paper requires you to listen to a selection of recorded material and answer the accompanying questions.

*There are four parts to the test, **One, Two, Three** and **Four**. You will hear Part Two **once** only. All the other parts of the test will be heard twice.*

There will be a pause before each part to allow you to look through the questions, and other pauses to let you think about your answers. At the end of every pause you will hear this sound.

tone

*You should write your answers on the **question** paper. You will have **ten** minutes at the end to **transfer your answers to the separate answer sheet**.*

The tape will now be stopped. You must ask any questions now as you will not be allowed to speak during the test.

[pause]

PART 1   *Now open your question paper and look at Part One.*

[pause]

Part One
You will hear a phone-in service called 'What's happening This Month'. For questions 1 to 10 look at the programme of events and fill in the information. You will hear the recording twice.

[pause]

tone

Announcer: Thank you for calling 'What's Happening This Month'. When the recording has finished, please replace your receiver. Should you wish to listen to the recording again, wait a few seconds and the information will be repeated.

The late Christian Donald's work still arouses great interest and this month sees the opening of an exhibition of his less well-known collection of portraits of his friends and celebrities. The exhibition entitled 'People I have known' will be held at International Studios. The entry fee is not cheap at ten pounds but a visit will make compulsive viewing for photo fanatics.

Boris Murimov, the great Russian artistic director, will be presenting 'As you like it' at the Theatre Royal in Central London. The production runs for two months before going on a world tour. A must for all lovers of Shakespeare!

The North Bank Theatre undertakes to stop those weekend blues with its season of classic greats entitled 'As They Were'. Saturday the 16th sees the start of the season and on Friday and Saturday evenings throughout the summer, a series of classic movies will be commanding the cinema screen. A real treat for cinema buffs!

A Festival of World Conservation will be held at the Media Centre, Bristol, on the 14th of this month. The main attraction will be 'The Disappearing Act', a film about the depletion of the world's resources followed by a debate about how to preserve our planet. There will be two guest speakers.

The Craft Council's touring exhibition 'Out of the Wood' takes trees as its theme. Jack Thompson's sculptures with leaves, Alison Wilson's furniture and Mark Gibb's giant fans are all on show. Catch them before the end of the month.

'Ways with Words' is a new Literature Festival to be held at the Dartington Centre in an area of outstanding natural beauty. The accommodation for guests on the week-long course is in a wonderful medieval building with stunning gardens. Guest speakers will include well-known writers speaking on such themes as 'Creating Utopias' and 'Soil and Toil'. Participation on a daily basis is also possible.

For further information about any of these events call 0273 – 616121.

[pause]

tone

Now you will hear the recording again.

[The recording is repeated.]

[pause]

That is the end of Part One.

[pause]

PART 2

Part Two
You will hear the representative of a travel company announcing changes to a holiday programme. For questions 11 to 16, write down where the events and activities will now take place.
Listen very carefully as you will hear the recording ONCE only.

[pause]

tone

Guide: Well, good afternoon ladies and gentlemen, on behalf of Pleasure Travel, may I welcome you to the beautiful resort of Budmouth. I'm sure you're really going to enjoy your stay here. And of course we've got so many exciting things for you to do here – you're really spoilt for choice, I'm afraid! Now could I just ask, have you all got your programmes? Good, fine, well perhaps I could just run through them with you. There are one or two little things we've had to change. No, really, hardly anything at all, in fact we've actually improved things, as I think you'll agree. So, I must just point out that *tomorrow* breakfast won't be served in the main dining room, but in the Red Room, so that we can have it all together because we need to make a punctual start for our excursion. Be in the foyer by 9.15 at the latest please, all ready for our coach trip to the Bicycle Museum. There's lots to see there and you can even ride some of the exhibits. And then, by popular request, some time to visit the newly renovated indoor market. You may remember that this was burnt down two years ago, but it's on our way and I know you all want to buy presents to take back with you. Then, although I know we said it'd be lunch in an *Italian* restaurant, we thought that, given the hot weather, it would be nice to eat out of doors so we've booked you in at an open-air restaurant. I've marked it on the town map that I'll be handing out in a minute. In the afternoon we'll be taking the river trip as on your programme but *not* visiting the old water mill – that's closed now unfortunately. And finally dinner back here in Budmouth, not in the hotel though, but at a restaurant we've only just discovered – 'The Wooden House' it's called, built entirely of wood as you might guess – and, of course, it's included in the price you've paid. Now, moving on to Day Two . . .

[pause]

That is the end of Part Two.

[pause]

PART 3

Part Three
You will hear a radio programme about taking family photographs. For questions 17 to 24, complete the notes. You will hear the recording twice.

[pause]

tone

Presenter: We all have drawers full of snapshots but what are they? A piece of history, a record of happy memories or a testament to the fact that the camera can indeed lie?

Gerald McGovern is a professional photographer. Jane France is one of the editors of a book called *The History of Domestic Photography*. Jane, as an art form, photography is really only just over a century old. How has it developed in domestic use?

Jane: Well, it's developed by being all of those things that you mentioned really. People are looking for pictures that will record their families and their homes and so the photographic technology has got closer and closer to the home – more and more informal. So if you look at the early pictures in people's albums – those taken when grandmother was a girl – in everybody's albums you'll find these very stiff, posed portraits, some of them studio portraits, and then you look at contemporary pictures today, you know, you find the family at play, you find snapshots which show children laughing, you find the holiday pictures, so it's changed over the years, become more relaxed, less of an ordeal.

Presenter: Gerald, is there a conflict, as there is in other artistic areas, between the low art of the domestic photographer and the high art of the professional?

Gerald: No, there's no conflict. I, as a professional photographer, don't take any family snaps because my children would never pose for me. In my commercial work, when I go and photograph other people's children, they have respect for the photographer. My kids never had any respect for me as a photographer at all. And if it hadn't been for my wife with her instamatic camera taking pictures, I wouldn't have any record at all of their younger years. I detect a sort of use now more by women using very easy to use, throw away cameras almost, and certainly in my family it seems to be the women who are taking the pictures rather than the men.

Jane: As Gerald says all the photographic companies, all the Kodak ads are directed at women. You know the kind of thing, even a woman can do this very simple photography. Taking pictures couldn't be easier these days.

Presenter: What about these ones then that you've got here? You've actually brought pictures that your wife has taken.

Gerald: Yes, these are not great photographs, but they are very important memories for me and they will be for my children – though they won't thank my wife for taking some of these poses. But it's interesting what you can do. The page here is a series of little cut-outs that my wife took. There's maybe twenty pictures here and they haven't all got great backgrounds. I mean, you were asking the difference between amateur and professional photography. Professional photography will have good backgrounds. Ruth would just go round and take pictures because they were good little fun moments and what she's done is cut out the best bits of it. She's got rid of, you know, the annoying chair in the background or whatever and just made one picture out of twenty bits of picture.

Presenter: But they're all lovely, smiling, oh, not that you haven't got lovely, smiling children, but does the camera in a way tell us lies about ourselves?

Gerald: You're right. People do play up to the camera and this is the greatest problem. Among this lot here, there aren't any pictures of children looking bad tempered. We do react to the camera. As soon as the camera comes out you sort of go into a pose, if you like. Probably that's their weakness really as family snaps.

Jane: Or is it a weakness? Isn't that just what they are? I mean . . .

Gerald: There's something missing. There's something missing from the family album. That is, anger, bad temper, you know the foul days, the sulks.

Presenter: Very briefly. What about video? Do you think it's taking over from the camera?

Gerald: I think so. And I think it's an interesting point. You know we were saying earlier about more women than men taking photos. Well, it'll be men that'll be making the videos.

Jane:	Because it's become hi-tech technology instead of the easy ...
Gerald:	And men are the only ones capable of doing it.
Jane:	In theory, in theory.
Gerald:	That's right.
Jane:	But in practice that's something that women, by becoming the recorders, I mean it's very much women who collected – it may have been the men in the early days that took the pictures, but very often, certainly we found that in the book it's the women that put the collections together. It's the women who've sort of made the history which they pass on.
Presenter:	Jane France, Gerald McGovern, thank you both very much.

[pause]

tone

Now you will hear the recording again.

[The recording is repeated.]

[pause]

That is the end of Part Three.

[pause]

PART 4   *Part Four*
This part consists of two tasks. You will hear five short extracts in which various people are talking about some aspect of travelling. Look at Task One. For questions 25 to 29, match the extracts as you hear them with the people listed A to H.

Now look at Task Two. For questions 30 to 34, match the extracts as you hear them with the phrases listed A to H that best describe each speaker's comment.

You will hear the recording twice. While you listen you must complete both tasks.

[pause]

tone

| Man: | Can't imagine why it takes you four hours – I mean, I can load up the samples, free offers and all the advertising literature, buzz up the motorway and be in the customer's office in three, and that's on a weekday! |

| Woman: | Obviously, planning any sort of military campaign involved sorting out communications – when you consider that London to Edinburgh was several days' forced march, rather than an hour by plane, before an army could begin to think about fighting. *Then* you begin to comprehend the difficulties of moving an army any distance at all, particularly when everything had to be carried on horseback! |

| Man: | They just don't think it can happen to them. It doesn't seem to matter how much is spent on trying to educate them, the idiots don't grasp it till they've had a smash. I |

never cease to be amazed at the speeds people do – they even overtake our patrol cars, so what can you expect?

Man: Well, of course, you expect them to be lively, we all were at that age. It's the mess they leave behind on the seats, under the seats, sweets and chewing gum, and half of them leave their books – I fill a rubbish bag twice a day with their junk. I remind them every morning when they get off to take their rubbish with them but it doesn't seem to make much difference.

Woman: Well, unfortunately as we all know, cities are violent places sometimes, especially for women. So we started this service, by women and for women, and we get more customers every day, people who want to have peace of mind, getting to and from work, to the airport, getting home from parties, well, everything really. What's more, we offer a fixed fare so they know what it's going to cost even before we set off.

[pause]

tone

Now you will hear the recording again. Remember, you must complete both tasks.

[The recording is repeated.]

[pause]

*That is the end of Part Four. There will now be a ten minute pause to allow you to **transfer your answers to the separate answer sheet**. Be sure to follow the numbering of all the questions. The question papers and answer sheets will then be collected by your supervisor.*

Teacher, pause the tape here for ten minutes. Remind your students when they have one minute left.

That is the end of the test.

Test 3 Key

Paper 1 Reading (1 hour 15 minutes)

Part 1

1 F   2 A   3 F   4 B   5 E   6 E   7 A   8 C   9 D
10 B   11 D   12 C   13 A   14 B   15 D   16 F

Part 2

17 C   18 G   19 B   20 H   21 D   22 F   23 A

Part 3

24 B   25 A   26 D   27 C   28 A

Part 4

29 F/H   30 F/H   31 C/H   32 C/H   33 A/C
34 A/C   35 E   36 B   37 H   38 A/G
39 A/G   40 G   41 E   42 D   43 B

Paper 2 Writing (2 hours)

Task-specific mark schemes

Question 1

Content (points covered)
Two letters
(a) Explain who they are and why they are writing. Refer to the original article, including date. Mention the inaccuracies in the article, e.g.: teachers not lazy; students do pass exams; excursions once a month with group rates; food inexpensive and of good quality. Should ask who the source of these inaccuracies is or at least refer to it obliquely. A positive attitude to KPD should be expressed. May ask for a correction to be printed though this is not necessary.
(b) A concise description of the action that has been taken and an expression of sympathy and support.
NB   Must attempt both the letter and the note for a minimum mark of 3.

Organisation and cohesion
(a) Letter format, though addresses not needed. Clear and appropriate introductory sentence. Paragraphs should follow a logical argument and the ideas should be organised appropriately. Strong conclusion.
(b) Brief – one paragraph.

128

Range
(a) language of complaint and disagreement. Expressions of indignation.
Vocabulary to do with aspects of school life.
(b) Polite expressions of sympathy and support. Some language of indignation.

Register
(a) Formal.
(b) Semi-informal. Likely to have quite a friendly tone. Register will be defined by the opening to the note e.g. 'Dear Mrs Driver' and must be consistent.

Target reader
(a) Would have an accurate picture of the school and would print a correction and/or an apology.
(b) Would be reassured and pleased to receive the note.

Question 2

Content (points covered)
Report should cover **two** magazines, clearly stating the first and second choices. Both magazines should be named and the content of each adequately outlined. It is up to the candidates to make the magazines chosen sound real. Clear reasons should be given as to why the magazines would be of benefit to students.
NB   Both content and benefits must be covered for a minimum mark of 3.

Organisation and cohesion
Report format, with information clearly set out. Suitable paragraphing – magazines can be dealt with separately or contrastively. Credit given for headings though these are not essential.
NB An introductory sentence in the form of a letter opening mentioning the competition is acceptable.

Range
Relevant vocabulary according to the magazines chosen.
Language of opinion and persuasion.

Register
Semi-formal or informal (for a college readership). Must be consistent.

Target reader
Would be informed about the magazines and be able to take a decision about them.

Question 3

Content (points covered)
Description of **three** videos of different types. Comments on why work colleagues or fellow-students might or might not want to watch them.
   (If only one video, maximum of 2 marks; if only two videos, maximum of 3 marks.)

Organisation and cohesion
Some review-type introduction.
Reasonably similar space given to each video.
Linking of video quality/effect on colleagues.

Range
Evidence of range in vocabulary in summarising videos and expressing feelings about them. Range of structures needed to make review interesting.

Register
Could be formal or informal according to magazine type (workplace, college) but tone should be consistent.

Target reader
Would be informed and have a clear idea whether each video would be worth watching or not.

Question 4

Content (points covered)
The directory is for students from abroad, who are 16+. Therefore, the entry should not merely be a description of the educational system. The country should be named and the information given of relevance to someone coming from abroad. Must cover 16+, and not just one sector. There should not be any introductory material on the SIMON directory, as this would be covered elsewhere in the book.
NB Penalise any excessive general material on the country concerned.

Organisation and cohesion
Clearly paragraphed and organised as a factual guide book type entry.

Range
Language of description and information. No personal opinions, though a positive description would be acceptable.

Register
Neutral or formal. Use of the first person singular verb forms inappropriate and the description should be impersonal.

Target reader
Would have a clear picture of what is available and know what action to take next.

Question 5

Content (points covered)
The job must be named or specific details about it given. Some description of the tasks involved in the job and the challenges.
NB 'Challenge' may be interpreted as opportunity or problem. A picture of the type of person best suited to the job. All three aspects of the task must be covered for a minimum of mark of 3.

It is not relevant to know why the person is leaving, so penalise if there is more than a brief reference to this.

Organisation and cohesion
Early reference to the job. Clear paragraphs. Headline or title an advantage.

Range
Vocabulary relating to that work area. Language of opinion.

Register
Register should be consistently informal or formal.

Target reader
Would be informed about the job and know whether it was suitable for them.

Paper 3 English in Use (1 hour 30 minutes)

Part 1

1 A   2 B   3 D   4 B   5 C   6 B   7 C   8 B   9 D
10 B   11 C   12 B   13 D   14 A   15 B

Part 2

16 an   17 can   18 one   19 any   20 have   21 when
22 but   23 This   24 which   25 while/whereas   26 as
27 ago   28 like   29 and   30 those

Part 3

31 ✓   32 roots   33 leaves   34 bark, a   35 ✓
36 names   37 'heartwood'   38 year's   39 rises in   40 ✓
41 contrast,   42 ✓   43 difference   44 cross-section
45 annual   46 their

Part 4

47 vacancies   48 consultants   49 applications/applicants
50 substantial   51 commitment   52 eagerness   53 package
54 closeness   55 spectacular   56 characterful/characteristic
57 rebuilt   58 stylistically   59 dominating   60 impressive
61 hesitation/hesitating

Part 5

62 make it/get   63 something/something else/another thing
64 leave   65 take part   66 a talk/a speech   67 the job/what

68 the end   **69** a waste   **70** enclosing   **71** a favour   **72** deal with
73 understand   **74** a ring/a call

Part 6

75 H   **76** C   **77** I   **78** D   **79** F   **80** B

Paper 4 Listening (45 minutes approximately)

Part 1

1 don't/won't have to/needn't   **2** one/one day (every Tuesday)
3 (a) taxi/(taxi)-cab   **4** not insured *or* not included in/covered by insurance
5 (£) 140 – (£) 365
6 clean (rooms)/do (any) cleaning/change the linen/clean up/do the cleaning up
7 (using) watersports equipment   **8** 5%/5 per cent less

Part 2

9 first settlement/primitive settlement/huts (on the hill top)
10 port/harbour (and) military camp/centre/base
11 (remains of) lighthouse/light house (on the hill)
12 Romans left/went away/withdrew/departed
13 wool trade/trade of/in wool *or* wool exports/exporting/exportation
14 (was) destroyed/flooded/washed away
15 reconstruction/rebuilding/(building) new town
16 coastline changed/town stranded/sea disappeared
17 (popular) tourist/touristic/tourism centre/place/town

Part 3

18 (study of) grain trade/economics/cereal/crop production (in tropical countries)
19 (local) guide (and) interpreter (*either order*)
20 relief/relieved/(was) glad/happy
21 walking/walked/on foot/waded/without boots/shoes/barefoot(ed)
22 snakes/snake bites
23 involvement/(very) involved/sympathy/sympathetic/concern/concerned/
    compassion/compassionate/pity
24 impressed
25 government (sells at a lower price)/government officials
26 (international) charities/charity workers
27 nervous/apprehensive/scared/no confidence/wasn't (very) confident/afraid/
    unconfident/insecure/insecurity

Part 4

28 D   **29** B   **30** G   **31** E   **32** F
33 A   **34** B   **35** F   **36** G   **37** H

Transcript   *This is the Cambridge Certificate in Advanced English Listening Test. Test Three.*

This paper requires you to listen to a selection of recorded material and answer the accompanying questions.

*There are four parts to the test, **One, Two, Three** and **Four**. You will hear Part Two **once** only. All the other parts of the test will be heard twice.*

There will be a pause before each part to allow you to look through the questions, and other pauses to let you think about your answers. At the end of every pause you will hear this sound.

tone

*You should write your answers on the **question** paper. You will have **ten** minutes at the end to **transfer your answers to the separate answer sheet.***

The tape will now be stopped. You must ask any questions now as you will not be allowed to speak during the test.

[pause]

PART 1   *Now open your question paper and look at Part One.*

[pause]

Part One
You will hear a travel company's information line recording giving details of its holidays in Crete. For questions 1 to 8, fill in the information. You will hear the recording twice.

[pause]

tone

Announcer: Welcome to our Cretan holiday information line. We thank you for calling and hope you have found something in our brochure to interest you. The following details might help you in your choice.

For those of you intending to fly direct to Crete from the UK, we would like to point out that all our flights operate on Tuesdays and we will be flying from Manchester, Newcastle and Heathrow airports to Heraklion or Chania airport in Crete. Transport to accommodation within 10 kilometres of the airports is free, but for those wishing to book a holiday further afield, we ask for a small supplement to cover the additional cost of the taxi fare.

An alternative is to hire a car, which can be collected at the airport. We must emphasise, however, that comprehensive insurance does not cover either the tyres or windscreen of the car and that, should you cause damage to any of these, you will be required to pay the full cost of repairs, so please drive carefully! Hiring a car costs anything between 140 and 365 pounds per week, depending on the season and type of car.

All our villas and apartments are self-catering with fridges and cookers, though it should be mentioned that the cookers are small and have only two or three rings. The majority of our villas and apartments are cleaned six times a week and the linen is changed once a week. Clients staying in some of our resorts may use the watersports equipment free of charge, and beginners' lessons, which can be paid for locally, are available every morning. On all our holidays we offer reductions for children aged eleven and under, and a five per cent reduction for senior citizens.

When you book we ask for a deposit of sixty pounds per person, plus insurance premium, as set out in our brochure.

If you would like more information, please ring us on 0501–5227.

Thank you for calling.

[pause]

tone

Now you will hear the recording again.

[The recording is repeated.]

[pause]

That is the end of Part One.

[pause]

PART 2

Part Two
You are on a tour of England and your coach has just arrived in Fancaster. The courier is telling you the history of the town before you explore it. For questions 9 to 17, complete the notes about the town. Listen very carefully as you will hear the recording ONCE only.

[pause]

tone

Courier:	Here we are in Fancaster. It's an historic place thousands of people visit every year. Let me tell you a bit about it before you explore. Do interrupt if there's anything you'd like to ask or don't understand. As you can see it's old, but 'How old is Fancaster?' people ask me. Well, it depends what you mean by Fancaster. In fact there was a very primitive settlement not far from where we are right now, between 2500 and 2250 BC.
Passenger:	How long ago?
Courier:	At the earliest 2500 and the latest 2250 BC, but it wasn't really a proper town, just huts on the hilltop, probably for defence.
Passenger:	How do we know?
Courier:	It was excavated a few years ago. Fancaster really started, as a recognisable sort of town, much later.
	As many of you may know the Romans arrived in Britain in the first century. Now, they built a harbour here in the first century, and also a military camp. It was quite important from the first till the fifth century.
Passenger:	Excuse me.
Courier:	Yes?
Passenger:	Can we see anything Roman?
Courier:	Yes, you can. There are some interesting remains of a lighthouse on the hill. The lighthouse was needed to guide ships, of course. Anyway, it was a kind of port and military camp for about three hundred years, and then in the fifth century the Romans went away and Fancaster almost disappeared for eight hundred years

after that. However, in the twelfth century there was a huge increase in the trade in wool and Fancaster grew rapidly as a wool exporting centre. And then there was a disaster. There was a great storm in 1287, and the town was destroyed when the sea flooded the whole town.

Passenger:	Excuse me? You mean the *whole* town ...
Courier:	Yes, the whole town was washed away. So they decided to go ahead with a new town on safer ground right here, and they actually started it in the early 14th century. About 1320, I believe. But the problem was after twenty years the coastline changed and left the town sort of stranded inland. The sea just disappeared. That was in the 1340s or so. So it was useless as a port and Fancaster was just a sleepy little place till recently. The medieval buildings have therefore survived very well, which is why it's such a popular tourist centre. I'm sure you'll enjoy strolling around. Please be back here by 12.30 because ...

[pause]

That is the end of Part Two.

[pause]

PART 3

Part Three
You will hear a radio interview with a university lecturer who was carrying out some research in a third world country when a flood disaster struck. For questions 18 to 27, complete the notes.

You will hear the recording twice.

[pause]

tone

Interviewer:	Dr Emily Gardiner is an economist from Lancashire University. She specialises in the study of cereal production in tropical areas and spends a great deal of time abroad. Recently she went on a two-week trip to study the grain trade in a third-world country where she experienced a flood disaster at first hand. Dr Gardiner, tell us what happened.
Dr Gardiner:	Well, when I was met at the airport, I was given a very tight timetable which involved travel to the provinces, all over the country in fact, although we started off in the capital. After about three or four days, my very good local guide and interpreter came with rather downcast faces and said that they didn't think we'd be able to go on our first trip to the East because the main city was waist-deep in water and the ferries that crossed the big rivers were unable to cross.
	So, we decided to go to the South instead. Now I'm rather glad that I never got there because the day after that, the main rail link was cut off and the lines were dangling limply into a really swollen river, which kept on rising.
Interviewer:	How did it affect you, I mean, were you marooned?
Dr Gardiner:	I was very lucky to be staying with a British family in the capital but the house where I was living was quite seriously affected.
	The first day the water rose about half a metre, and the children paddled in it. Worms fled from it but were finally drowned and then eaten by big black ants which invaded the house.
Interviewer:	Were you able to get around? Did you have to take a boat?
Dr Gardiner:	No, I waded, well walked around actually, without any shoes! At first I was told that

	I was a fool because of snakes and, of course a lot of the deaths there have been because of snake bites. But we were quite a long way from the rice-fields where the snakes abound, so I bargained on the fact that there wouldn't be too many!
Interviewer:	You were, as you say, staying in a rich area of the capital, did you see what was happening in the poorer areas?
Dr Gardiner:	I did indeed, and I felt very involved with it because we could see what was happening on the lower ground. The houses are really like tents made of rush matting supported by bamboo poles and as the flood water gets deeper, people are forced to move to higher and higher land taking their houses with them.
Interviewer:	And what about food supplies?
Dr Gardiner:	Well, I was of course studying the merchants and it was quite impressive how they had managed to move all their stock well above flood level and were able to double prices in some areas of the capital that were cut off. The price of grain varied by about a hundred percent, depending on where you were in the city. Now what the Government tries to do in these circumstances is two things: one is to try to sell some of its stock on the open market at low prices in a vain effort to bring down prices, and the other thing is to organise relief and soup kitchens in conjunction with the international charities.
Interviewer:	How did you manage to get out because the airport was under water for a lot of the time and there just weren't any flights?
Dr Gardiner:	I, of course, double reconfirmed my ticket out. But on the day itself I was told that the flight didn't exist and really only got out because there was a spare seat on another flight. As we taxied for take-off, the wings of the F28, which is by no means a large plane, were actually over the flood waters on the runway, which didn't inspire a great deal of confidence. So it was one of the most spirited take-offs I've ever had.
Interviewer:	But you lived to tell the tale.
Dr Gardiner:	Yes.

[pause]

tone

Now you will hear the recording again.

[The recording is repeated.]

[pause]

That is the end of Part Three.

[pause]

PART 4

Part Four
This part consists of two tasks. You will hear various people talking about education. Look at Task One. For questions 28 to 32, match the extracts as you hear them with the people listed A to H.

Now look at Task Two. For questions 33 to 37, match the extracts as you hear them with each speaker's intention listed A to H.

You will hear the recording twice. While you listen you must complete both tasks.

[pause]

tone

Parent:

What we really need to know is how hard to push her. We neither of us went to college ourselves, and we don't really know how much work they have to do. Is she doing enough homework? It seems like a lot to us, but as I say, we can't tell.

Politician:

The thing that concerns me is that higher education is not fitting young people for the world in which they are going to find themselves. It's no use their dreaming up fancy policies if they produce too many teachers and not enough mechanics. They should be more in touch with the real world: turning out people to fit jobs we want done in the manufacturing industries. We can't be expected to turn in a profit if we can't get the labour with the right skills.

Museum guide:

When I started, I thought they'd be difficult to handle, wandering about, trying to fiddle with things, touching the things on display. Actually, they're usually very well behaved. And they're much better informed than most members of the public. It's often a visit that ties in with a history project and sometimes I help the teacher prepare worksheets. They ask some difficult questions, too, sometimes. It's quite challenging, in a pleasant sort of way.

Sports coach:

Well, we do sometimes get a youngster coming in from his school with glowing reports about how many junior records he's broken and so on. But we don't take too much notice of that. What we do is, we put everyone through three months of intensive training, mainly to get rid of all the bad habits they've picked up, and see they're really fit, and then we start selection and specialisation after that. We find it works very well.

University professor:

I know you've all been wondering about the details for next week. Well, I can now tell you that the Education Minister herself will be on the campus for most of the day on Wednesday, and she will be spending part of the morning in this faculty, looking in on some lectures and having coffee with us here in the common room. I myself will be lunching with her along with other department heads and the senior administrative staff.

[pause]

tone

Now you will hear the recording again. Remember, you must complete both tasks.

[The recording is repeated.]

[pause]

*That is the end of Part Four. There will now be a ten minute pause to allow you to **transfer your answers to the separate answer sheet.** Be sure to follow the numbering of all the questions. The question papers and answer sheets will then be collected by your supervisor.*

Teacher, pause the tape here for ten minutes. Remind your students when they have one minute left.

That is the end of the test.

Test 4 Key

Paper 1   Reading (1 hour 15 minutes)

Part 1

1 D   2 C   3 G   4 B   5 C   6 B   7 E   8 G
9 B   10 F   11 G   12 A   13 H

Part 2

14 E   15 C   16 F   17 A   18 H   19 D   20 G

Part 3

21 A   22 B   23 A   24 D   25 C

Part 4

26 E   27 G   28 H   29 A   30 H/J   31 H/J
32 E/F   33 E/F   34 B/C/D   35 B/C/D   36 B/C/D
37 D   38 F   39 C   40 J   41 A/I   42 A/I

Paper 2 Writing (2 hours)

Task-specific mark schemes

Question 1

Content (points covered)
Explain who they are and why they are writing.
Say why changes are needed – refer to the September programme and to all five
problems in the notes. Give at least two or three suggestions for future
activities, to be taken from the notes, indicating why they would be successful.
Do not penalise if all nine are included.
Tactful ending.
Penalise lifting with expansion.

Organisation and cohesion
Carefully worded introduction.
One or more paragraphs on why changes are needed. Several possible ways of
organising the letter:
• suggestions in one paragraph and reasons why following
• suggestions incorporated into outline of problems
• each suggestion with reason in a separate paragraph.

Range
Expressions of opinion, suggestion and tact.
Specific vocabulary relating to the suggestions and existing programme topics.

Register
Semi-formal – the club has a 'friendly atmosphere', so overly formal writing
would not be appropriate (though the chairperson is probably an older person).

Target reader
Chairperson of the club should feel they have received constructive criticism
and would take action to revitalise the club.

Question 2
Content (points covered)
Description of how a specified strike (a **general** strike acceptable) has affected
one aspect of local life.
Reference to exaggerated reports.
Reassuring account of how people are coping (goes down to the next band if
reassurance omitted).

Organisation and cohesion
Letter format, with introductory greeting and closing remark; bulk of letter
clearly set out in paragraphs.

Range
Some specific vocabulary used to summarise effects of the strike; effective
criticism of media coverage.

Register
Informal.

Target reader
Would feel informed and reassured.

Question 3
Content (points covered)
Recent improvements in facilities for visitors.
Detailed description which may include how things used to be in contrast to
how they are now.
NB No irrelevant paragraphs about sun, scenery, etc!

Organisation and cohesion
Clear paragraphing, with lead-in and conclusion appropriate to article style.

Range
Language of comparison and contrast.
Original phrases for describing improvement.
Specific vocabulary for facilities e.g. relating to hotels, culture, travel.

Register
Consistently formal or informal according to type of magazine envisaged.

Target reader
Would feel informed and interested.

Question 4
Content (points covered)
Brief description of series – not appropriate to dwell on plot/content; should state title of series.
Other reasons why people should watch the series.
Positive encouragement to watch regularly.

Organisation and cohesion
Introductory paragraph on the series.
Clear focus to the argument, with separate paragraphs stating each reason.
Ending should be fairly forceful.

Range
Language of opinion and recommendation.
Vocabulary relevant to TV productions.

Register
Semi-formal review – aimed at colleagues.

Target reader
Should feel informed and enthused about the series.

Question 5
Content (points covered)
Types of employment available to school leavers in local area.
Pay and conditions.
Training possibilities.
Reference to young people's problems/opportunities in the job market.
NB Do not penalise if university graduates referred to.

Organisation and cohesion
Well-organised report. Credit for clear layout, e.g. use of headings.

Range
Description and comment.
Specialist vocabulary relating to work.

Register
Formal, impersonal report style.

Target reader
Should feel informed.

Paper 3 **English in Use** (1 hour 30 minutes)

Part 1

1 C   2 D   3 B   4 C   5 B   6 D   7 A   8 B
9 C   10 D   11 C   12 B   13 D   14 A   15 B

Part 2

16 Although/Though   17 the   18 such/this   19 just/now
20 who/that   21 while/when/whilst   22 after/during   23 to
24 another   25 on   26 with/by   27 to   28 However
29 so   30 even

Part 3

31 as   32 been   33 with   34 the   35 only   36 ✓
37 all   38 ✓   39 for   40 ✓   41 are   42 ✓   43 ✓
44 both   45 to   46 be

Part 4

47 reliable   48 knowledgeable   49 explanations
50 comparison   51 satisfactory   52 biased   53 publication
54 saddest   55 hopelessly   56 inefficient   57 impatient
58 guaranteeing   59 disapproval   60 importance
61 appearance

Part 5

62 it out   63 your own   64 quickly/swiftly/promptly   65 soon as
66 stop/put down   67 get out   68 Check/Find/Identify
69 (should) find   70 outside of   71 think about   72 go back
73 safe/OK/all right/alright/permitted   74 are told/are informed

Part 6

75 B   76 I   77 D   78 E   79 C   80 H

Paper 4 **Listening** (45 minutes approximately)

Part 1

1 Business Matters   2 graphic design agency   3 six/6
4 interviewed   5 350 words
6 (business) colleague/relative/related/family
7 daytime phone/tel/number/no   8 June 15
9 September's/(the) September

Part 2

10 Science Park   11 flooding/floods/heavy rain/thunderstorm
12 season tickets   13 blocked/jammed/impassable
14 cancellation to flights   15 delayed
16 traffic delays/jams/holdups/congestion

Part 3

17 C   18 B   19 D   20 A   21 B   22 D

Part 4

23 B   24 A   25 C   26 A   27 C

28 A   29 B   30 B   31 A   32 C

Transcript

This is the Cambridge Certificate in Advanced English Listening Test. Test Four.

This paper requires you to listen to a selection of recorded material and answer the accompanying questions.

*There are four parts to the test, **One**, **Two**, **Three** and **Four**. You will hear Part Two **once** only. All the other parts of the test will be heard twice.*

There will be a pause before each part to allow you to look through the questions, and other pauses to let you think about your answers. At the end of every pause you will hear this sound.

tone

*You should write your answers on the **question** paper. You will have **ten minutes at the end to transfer your answers to the separate answer sheet.***

The tape will now be stopped. You must ask any questions now as you will not be allowed to speak during the test.

[pause]

PART 1

[*Now open your question paper and look at Part One.*]

[pause]

Part One
You will hear part of a radio programme in which details of a competition are announced. For questions 1 to 9, complete the notes. You will hear the recording twice.

[pause]

tone

Presenter: ... and it's at this point in the programme that we come to the details of our annual competition. We want to hear from you if you're aged between eighteen and twenty-five years of age and you've started up your own business in the last year. Here on 'Business Matters' we're looking for a young man or a woman to win our 'Young Entrepreneur' award. Last year you may remember it was awarded to Yunus Ozal from Turkey who set up his own highly successful graphic design agency and now employs a staff of fifteen from his office based in Ankara. But we had entries from all over the world and all kinds of business enterprises. Keeping bees to microlighting; jewellery-making to fast food. We shortlisted six people out of more than three hundred entries and then sent our reporters to interview each finalist to tell us in more detail how they had gone about raising capital, finding premises, advertising their business and impacting on the market.

Here's what you have to do. Send in your entry – it must be typed, on one side of the paper only – and tell us how you got your business enterprise off the ground. Maybe you employ other people, maybe you run it single-handed. Maybe you're small but growing. Maybe you're already into the export market.

Make it interesting reading! Remember we have to read through hundreds of entries and you'll want yours to be a memorable one in the minds of the judges. Keep your entry within 350 words. And when it's complete, get an independent witness to verify your entry by signing their name and occupation at the end. This must be someone who is not related to you and who is not a business colleague but who has known you for at least three years.

Don't forget to add your full name and address, the name and address of your business and give us your daytime phone number so that we can contact you if we need to. The closing date for entries is three months from now – that's June fifteen. If you want your entry returned eventually then send us an envelope addressed to yourself and enclose an international reply coupon. We'll be broadcasting the shortlisted entries the second week in July so stay tuned to 'Business Matters'. The name of the prizewinner will be announced two months after that, in September. Send your entries to 'Business Matters', Post Office Box 171 . . .

[pause]

tone

Now you will hear the recording again.

[The recording is repeated.]

[pause]

That is the end of Part One.

[pause]

PART 2

Part Two
You will hear a local radio broadcast about transport and travel. For questions 10 to 16, complete the notes using no more than three words in each gap. Listen very carefully as you will hear the recording ONCE only.

[pause]

tone

Announcer: And now at five to seven, today's round-up of the travel blackspots. And I'm afraid quite a few of you are going to experience some problems getting to work this morning. I'll begin with delays caused by roadworks. First of all, motorists heading for the Science Park are likely to be delayed on the approach road as there are roadworks with temporary traffic lights just half a mile from the Science Park entrance.

Next, bad news for commuters who use Stadley Station. The thunderstorms over the weekend have caused flooding which could be dangerous, so the station has had to be closed until the water can be pumped away. One ray of light is that commuters with season tickets will be able to use them on special buses between seven and nine in the morning, which will run from outside the station into the city centre until the flooding has been dealt with, so if you're a regular, it shouldn't mean too much of a problem.

In Chorley village centre an articulated lorry has collided with a tanker on the main road, which is likely to remain impassable for some hours. The only advice at the moment is to steer well clear of Chorley this morning if you can, as there are no diversions, so, traffic queues will be severe until the road can be cleared.

At the airport, I'm glad to say, both internal and international flights are operating and there are no cancellations notified, in spite of the recent bad weather. However, I should warn you that delays are extremely likely on a number of international flights. Advice to travellers going abroad is to check in as normal, but take a good fat book just in case, I'm afraid.

Lastly, right in the centre of the city, there are problems on most roads. This is on account of the bomb scare during the night in Central Square. The area which was cordoned off has now been opened up, within the last half hour in fact, but traffic jams have already built up and are unlikely to clear before the end of the rush hour.

Well, in spite of all that, I hope your journey today isn't too terrible. Now to take us up to the news at seven, here is Gerry Morton with today's local weather outlook ...

[pause]

That is the end of Part Two.

[pause]

PART 3

Part Three
You will hear part of a radio programme about dancing. For questions 17 to 22, choose the correct answer A, B, C or D.

You will hear the recording twice.

[pause]

tone

Presenter:	Most of us dance at some time or other, but do you ever wonder why? What is it that makes us dance? In this report, that's what I'm looking into and I started at a night club, where I put that question to Shirley, who was just taking a break from the dance floor.
Shirley:	It all happens automatically. I don't know the scientific process but it's all to do with the rhythm. I mean, when you hear that drum and bass sound ... you know ... the hips start moving and the next thing you know you're dancing. You just feel like it and you have to get up and go with it. I mean, I'll dance to anything. I like everything from the latest sounds right back to the Fifties' rock'n'roll, as long as it's cheerful music.
Presenter:	The music is obviously a major factor in making people dance, but is it possible to predict what kind of music a particular crowd will dance to? I asked Tony Leach, who for twenty years has been the leader of a dance band who play at parties, weddings and other social gatherings.
Tony:	The time that I decide what our first song is going to be is approximately five seconds before we start it. I look around and I think yes, it feels like a slow song or

an old rock'n'roll song or a romantic ballad is right. Sometimes I change my mind later, though.

I might get to the end of a song thinking that we'll do a particular one next and then I see their physical attitudes on the dance floor and I think, 'No, wrong' and instantly swap to something else. Sometimes the way people react to a certain song will tell you a lot about the sorts of things they're going to dance to for the rest of the night.

Presenter: So creating the right mood is essential, but according to Tony, what makes us dance can also depend on other things.

Tony: Different social groups have different social rules. There are occasions where it's the done thing to dance and so it almost doesn't matter what's played. Then at other times, perhaps at company dances, you get people who are embarrassed about dancing in front of bosses. So there's one great social divide, which is between people who think you go onto the dance floor in order to make polite conversation with your partner and people who go onto the dance floor to fling their bodies around in time to music.

Presenter: Emma Phillips, a music journalist, thinks that dancing plays a very significant role in the lives of young people in particular.

Emma: There's a massive club scene going on. These kids, they need to release energy and they're doing it by dancing to their own kind of music. I mean, every generation needs its own soundtrack, one that just belongs to them.

Presenter: Emma believes, however, that what gets us on our feet depends not just on age but is also rooted deep within our cultural background.

Emma: I think dancing does break down the barriers but it also reveals some of the barriers. By the very fact that some people only dance to a certain kind of music, that reveals something about them, maybe their social background, you know, whereas other people might get up and dance to anything, which means they're a bit more open-minded about what's going on around them.

Presenter: So, finally, I asked both Tony and Emma, how they would sum up dancing.

Emma: If you look around the world, dance has been a very fulfilling, uplifting and spiritual thing from the beginning of time.

Tony: I think dancing should be seen as a physical reaction to music in a social situation. As long as people are happy then things like embarrassment just don't apply. I think it's the most amazing phenomenon. You only have to play the right music in the right situation and people get on the dance floor. I think it's a basic human instinct.

Presenter: And you might like to know that Tony and his band, The Kings of Swing, will be featured on Radio 2 this evening at 8.30.

[pause]

tone

Now you will hear the recording again.

[The recording is repeated.]

[pause]

That is the end of Part Three.

[pause]

PART 4   *Part Four*

You will hear five short extracts in which different people are talking about performances that they have been to. For questions 23 to 32, choose the correct answer A, B or C.

You will hear the recording twice.

[pause]

tone

Woman: A friend of mine phoned up at the last minute and asked me if I wanted to go to this show. It was being put on by a group of South African singers who were touring this country for four weeks. My friend had heard they were brilliant and this would be the last chance to see them before they returned home. Well, when we arrived what struck me most was that the stage was completely bare, apart from a few microphone stands. And when they started, it was incredible. I've never really heard anything like it before. They just stood and sang and all the orchestral noises like drums and violin sounds they just made with their voices. I was completely spell-bound from beginning to end.

Man: I'd been looking forward to this show for a long time. I used to be a big fan of James Hopper many years ago. I was hoping he'd do all the old familiar songs and I think the rest of the audience were too. The thing was, the rest of the band were completely out of time. They just kept losing the rhythm and some of the old songs were almost unrecognisable. It didn't help that you couldn't hear his guitar very well and all the voices were a bit distorted. But the audience couldn't get enough of it. They shouted their heads off – cheering and clapping. I was a bit disappointed though.

Woman: This was an interesting experience. For a start, the theatre was in *Pelman Street*. Now I've walked up and down that street many times, but I never realised there was a theatre there. It was very intimate – it only holds a maximum of forty people. The show was a big success up in London last year, huge audiences, but unfortunately only a handful of people turned up for the performance *here*. I'm not surprised though – it was rather amateurish. They could have done with using at least a bit of make-up and learning their parts better. They relied on covering up their mistakes by really throwing themselves into their characters.

Man: This was one of the few classical concerts that I decided to go to. As I sat there in the audience waiting for the performance to begin, I spotted quite a few of my colleagues who I hadn't realised appreciated that type of music. We sat there for quite a while because the concert was delayed for some reason. When the orchestra finally trooped in, I noticed that one of the trumpeters was Mary Brownlow who I'd been to school with. I was amazed because I never realised she was at all musical. But then I remembered that she did play the drums when she was younger and I think her brother played the violin. Unfortunately, Mary didn't play very well and made quite a few mistakes, especially in the first piece.

Woman: Well, I thought I'd go to the circus. My friend has a couple of kids who were keen to see it and they invited me along. I quite enjoyed it really, even though it tied up a whole afternoon. There were no animals, just clowns, acrobats, people throwing burning sticks in the air – you know the kind of thing. I think the acrobats made the greatest impact. They must train incredibly hard to achieve such levels of fitness. The whole show lasted a couple of hours which was about right, but I think we would have gone to the later show if it hadn't been for the kids.

[pause]

tone

Now you will hear the recording again.

[The recording is repeated.]

[pause]

*That is the end of Part Four. There will now be a ten minute pause to allow you to **transfer your answers to the separate answer sheet.** Be sure to follow the numbering of all the questions. The question papers and answer sheets will then be collected by your supervisor.*

Teacher, pause the tape here for ten minutes. Remind your students when they have one minute left.

That is the end of the test.

UNIVERSITY *of* CAMBRIDGE
Local Examinations Syndicate

SAMPLE

Candidate Name
If not already printed, write name
in CAPITALS and complete the
Candidate No. grid (in pencil).

Candidate's signature

- -

Examination Title

Centre

Supervisor:

[X] If the candidate is ABSENT or has WITHDRAWN shade here ▭

Centre No.

Candidate No.

**Examination
Details**

0	0	0	0
1	1	1	1
2	2	2	2
3	3	3	3
4	4	4	4
5	5	5	5
6	6	6	6
7	7	7	7
8	8	8	8
9	9	9	9

Multiple-choice Answer Sheet

Use a pencil   Mark one letter for each question.

For example:

If you think C is the right answer to the
question, mark your answer sheet like this:

Change your answer
like this:

1	A B C D E F G H I
2	A B C D E F G H I
3	A B C D E F G H I
4	A B C D E F G H I
5	A B C D E F G H I
6	A B C D E F G H I
7	A B C D E F G H I
8	A B C D E F G H I
9	A B C D E F G H I
10	A B C D E F G H I
11	A B C D E F G H I
12	A B C D E F G H I
13	A B C D E F G H I
14	A B C D E F G H I
15	A B C D E F G H I
16	A B C D E F G H I
17	A B C D E F G H I
18	A B C D E F G H I
19	A B C D E F G H I
20	A B C D E F G H I

21	A B C D E F G H I
22	A B C D E F G H I
23	A B C D E F G H I
24	A B C D E F G H I
25	A B C D E F G H I
26	A B C D E F G H I
27	A B C D E F G H I
28	A B C D E F G H I
29	A B C D E F G H I
30	A B C D E F G H I
31	A B C D E F G H I
32	A B C D E F G H I
33	A B C D E F G H I
34	A B C D E F G H I
35	A B C D E F G H I
36	A B C D E F G H I
37	A B C D E F G H I
38	A B C D E F G H I
39	A B C D E F G H I
40	A B C D E F G H I

41	A B C D E F G H I
42	A B C D E F G H I
43	A B C D E F G H I
44	A B C D E F G H I
45	A B C D E F G H I
46	A B C D E F G H I
47	A B C D E F G H I
48	A B C D E F G H I
49	A B C D E F G H I
50	A B C D E F G H I
51	A B C D E F G H I
52	A B C D E F G H I
53	A B C D E F G H I
54	A B C D E F G H I
55	A B C D E F G H I
56	A B C D E F G H I
57	A B C D E F G H I
58	A B C D E F G H I
59	A B C D E F G H I
60	A B C D E F G H I

SAMPLE

Candidate Name
If not already printed, write name
in CAPITALS and complete the
Candidate No. grid (in pencil).

Candidate's signature

- -

Examination Title

Centre

Supervisor:

[X] If the candidate is ABSENT or has WITHDRAWN shade here ⊂⊃

Centre No.

Candidate No.

**Examination
Details**

0	0	0	0
1	1	1	1
2	2	2	2
3	3	3	3
4	4	4	4
5	5	5	5
6	6	6	6
7	7	7	7
8	8	8	8
9	9	9	9

Candidate Answer Sheet

Use a pencil

For **Parts 1** and **6**:
Mark ONE letter for each question.
For example, if you think **B** is the
right answer to the question,
mark your answer sheet like this:

For **Parts 2, 3, 4** and **5**:
Write your answers in the spaces
next to the numbers like this:

| 0 | A B̲ C D |

| 0 | *example* |

Part 1				
1	A	B	C	D
2	A	B	C	D
3	A	B	C	D
4	A	B	C	D
5	A	B	C	D
6	A	B	C	D
7	A	B	C	D
8	A	B	C	D
9	A	B	C	D
10	A	B	C	D
11	A	B	C	D
12	A	B	C	D
13	A	B	C	D
14	A	B	C	D
15	A	B	C	D

Part 2	Do not write here
16	⊂⊃ 16 ⊂⊃
17	⊂⊃ 17 ⊂⊃
18	⊂⊃ 18 ⊂⊃
19	⊂⊃ 19 ⊂⊃
20	⊂⊃ 20 ⊂⊃
21	⊂⊃ 21 ⊂⊃
22	⊂⊃ 22 ⊂⊃
23	⊂⊃ 23 ⊂⊃
24	⊂⊃ 24 ⊂⊃
25	⊂⊃ 25 ⊂⊃
26	⊂⊃ 26 ⊂⊃
27	⊂⊃ 27 ⊂⊃
28	⊂⊃ 28 ⊂⊃
29	⊂⊃ 29 ⊂⊃
30	⊂⊃ 30 ⊂⊃

Turn
over for
parts
3 - 6
→

149

SAMPLE

Part 3		Do not write here
31		31
32		32
33		33
34		34
35		35
36		36
37		37
38		38
39		39
40		40
41		41
42		42
43		43
44		44
45		45
46		46

Part 4		Do not write here
47		47
48		48
49		49
50		50
51		51
52		52
53		53
54		54
55		55
56		56
57		57
58		58
59		59
60		60
61		61

Part 5		Do not write here
62		62
63		63
64		64
65		65
66		66
67		67
68		68
69		69
70		70
71		71
72		72
73		73
74		74

Part 6								
75	A	B	C	D	E	F	G	H	I
76	A	B	C	D	E	F	G	H	I
77	A	B	C	D	E	F	G	H	I
78	A	B	C	D	E	F	G	H	I
79	A	B	C	D	E	F	G	H	I
80	A	B	C	D	E	F	G	H	I

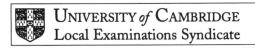

UNIVERSITY *of* CAMBRIDGE
Local Examinations Syndicate

SAMPLE

Candidate Name
If not already printed, write name
in CAPITALS and complete the
Candidate No. grid (in pencil).

Candidate's signature --

Examination Title

Centre

Supervisor:

[X] If the candidate is ABSENT or has WITHDRAWN shade here ⊏⊐

Centre No.

Candidate No.

Examination Details

0	0	0	0
1	1	1	1
2	2	2	2
3	3	3	3
4	4	4	4
5	5	5	5
6	6	6	6
7	7	7	7
8	8	8	8
9	9	9	9

Listening Comprehension Answer Sheet

Enter the test number here ☐☐☐

For office use only ⊏3⊐ CPE ⊏5⊐ CAE ⊏0⊐⊏1⊐⊏2⊐⊏3⊐⊏4⊐⊏5⊐⊏6⊐⊏7⊐⊏8⊐⊏9⊐
⊏0⊐⊏1⊐⊏2⊐⊏3⊐⊏4⊐⊏5⊐⊏6⊐⊏7⊐⊏8⊐⊏9⊐

Write your answers below	Do not write here		Continue here	Do not write here
1	⊏⊐ 1 ⊏⊐		21	⊏⊐ 21 ⊏⊐
2	⊏⊐ 2 ⊏⊐		22	⊏⊐ 22 ⊏⊐
3	⊏⊐ 3 ⊏⊐		23	⊏⊐ 23 ⊏⊐
4	⊏⊐ 4 ⊏⊐		24	⊏⊐ 24 ⊏⊐
5	⊏⊐ 5 ⊏⊐		25	⊏⊐ 25 ⊏⊐
6	⊏⊐ 6 ⊏⊐		26	⊏⊐ 26 ⊏⊐
7	⊏⊐ 7 ⊏⊐		27	⊏⊐ 27 ⊏⊐
8	⊏⊐ 8 ⊏⊐		28	⊏⊐ 28 ⊏⊐
9	⊏⊐ 9 ⊏⊐		29	⊏⊐ 29 ⊏⊐
10	⊏⊐ 10 ⊏⊐		30	⊏⊐ 30 ⊏⊐
11	⊏⊐ 11 ⊏⊐		31	⊏⊐ 31 ⊏⊐
12	⊏⊐ 12 ⊏⊐		32	⊏⊐ 32 ⊏⊐
13	⊏⊐ 13 ⊏⊐		33	⊏⊐ 33 ⊏⊐
14	⊏⊐ 14 ⊏⊐		34	⊏⊐ 34 ⊏⊐
15	⊏⊐ 15 ⊏⊐		35	⊏⊐ 35 ⊏⊐
16	⊏⊐ 16 ⊏⊐		36	⊏⊐ 36 ⊏⊐
17	⊏⊐ 17 ⊏⊐		37	⊏⊐ 37 ⊏⊐
18	⊏⊐ 18 ⊏⊐		38	⊏⊐ 38 ⊏⊐
19	⊏⊐ 19 ⊏⊐		39	⊏⊐ 39 ⊏⊐
20	⊏⊐ 20 ⊏⊐		40	⊏⊐ 40 ⊏⊐